GLOBAL VIEWPOINTS

Capital Punishment

JAN 13

CH

Other Books of Related Interest:

Current Controversies Series

Prisons

Torture

Introducing Issues with Opposing Viewpoints Series

The Death Penalty

Death and Dying

Euthanasia

Prisons

Opposing Viewpoints Series

Criminal Justice

Organ Donation

Euthanasia

Prisons

GLOBALVIEWPOINTS

Capital Punishment

Noah Berlatsky, Book Editor

GREENHAVEN PRESS
A part of Gale, Cengage Learning

GALE
CENGAGE Learning

Detroit • New York • San Francisco • New Haven, Conn • Waterville, Maine • London

Christine Nasso, *Publisher*
Elizabeth Des Chenes, *Managing Editor*

© 2010 Greenhaven Press, a part of Gale, Cengage Learning

Gale and Greenhaven Press are registered trademarks used herein under license.

For more information, contact:
Greenhaven Press
27500 Drake Rd.
Farmington Hills, MI 48331-3535
Or you can visit our Internet site at gale.cengage.com

For product information and technology assistance, contact us at

Gale Customer Support, 1-800-877-4253
For permission to use material from this text or product, submit all requests online at www.cengage.com/permissions

Further permissions questions can be emailed to permissionrequest@cengage.com

Articles in Greenhaven Press anthologies are often edited for length to meet page requirements. In addition, original titles of these works are changed to clearly present the main thesis and to explicitly indicate the author's opinion. Every effort is made to ensure that Greenhaven Press accurately reflects the original intent of the authors. Every effort has been made to trace the owners of copyrighted material.

Cover image © F. Carter Smith/Sygma/Corbis

LIBRARY OF CONGRESS CATALOGING-IN-PUBLICATION DATA

Capital punishment / Noah Berlatsky, book editor.
  p. cm. -- (Global viewpoints)
Includes bibliographical references and index.
ISBN 978-0-7377-4663-1 (hardcover)
ISBN 978-0-7377-4664-8 (pbk.)
1. Capital punishment--Juvenile literature. 2. Capital punishment--Cross-cultural studies--Juvenile literature. I. Berlatsky, Noah.
HV8694.C2845 2010
364.66--dc22

                                                        2009040117

Printed in the United States of America
   2 3 4 5 6   16 15 14 13 12

FD187

Contents

Chapter 1: Capital Punishment and Morality

Chapter 2: Capital Punishment and Public Opinion

Chapter 3: Capital Punishment and Justice

Chapter 4: Capital Punishment and International Relations

Foreword

*"The problems of all of humanity can
only be solved by all of humanity."*
—*Swiss author Friedrich Dürrenmatt*

Global interdependence has become an undeniable reality. Mass media and technology have increased worldwide access to information and created a society of global citizens. Understanding and navigating this global community is a challenge, requiring a high degree of information literacy and a new level of learning sophistication.

Building on the success of its flagship series, *Opposing Viewpoints,* Greenhaven Press has created the *Global Viewpoints* series to examine a broad range of current, often controversial topics of worldwide importance from a variety of international perspectives. Providing students and other readers with the information they need to explore global connections and think critically about worldwide implications, each *Global Viewpoints* volume offers a panoramic view of a topic of widespread significance.

Drugs, famine, immigration—a broad, international treatment is essential to do justice to social, environmental, health, and political issues such as these. Junior high, high school, and early college students, as well as general readers, can all use *Global Viewpoints* anthologies to discern the complexities relating to each issue. Readers will be able to examine unique national perspectives while, at the same time, appreciating the interconnectedness that global priorities bring to all nations and cultures.

Material in each volume is selected from a diverse range of sources, including journals, magazines, newspapers, nonfiction books, speeches, government documents, pamphlets, organization newsletters, and position papers. *Global Viewpoints* is truly global, with material drawn primarily from international sources available in English and secondarily from U.S. sources with extensive international coverage.

Features of each volume in the *Global Viewpoints* series include:

- An **annotated table of contents** that provides a brief summary of each essay in the volume, including the name of the country or area covered in the essay.

- An **introduction** specific to the volume topic.

- A **world map** to help readers locate the countries or areas covered in the essays.

- For each viewpoint, an **introduction** that contains notes about the author and source of the viewpoint explains why material from the specific country is being presented, summarizes the main points of the viewpoint, and offers three **guided reading questions** to aid in understanding and comprehension.

- **For further discussion** questions that promote critical thinking by asking the reader to compare and contrast aspects of the viewpoints or draw conclusions about perspectives and arguments.

- A worldwide list of **organizations to contact** for readers seeking additional information.

- A **periodical bibliography** for each chapter and a **bibliography of books** on the volume topic to aid in further research.

- A comprehensive **subject index** to offer access to people, places, events, and subjects cited in the text, with the countries covered in the viewpoints highlighted.

Global Viewpoints is designed for a broad spectrum of readers who want to learn more about current events, history, political science, government, international relations, economics, environmental science, world cultures, and sociology—students doing research for class assignments or debates, teachers and faculty seeking to supplement course materials, and others wanting to understand current issues better. By presenting how people in various countries perceive the root causes, current consequences, and proposed solutions to worldwide challenges, *Global Viewpoints* volumes offer readers opportunities to enhance their global awareness and their knowledge of cultures worldwide.

Introduction

"I watched a man die once. There was no question that everyone concerned knew this to be a dreadful unnatural action. I believe it is always the same—the whole jail, wardens and prisoners alike are up-set when there is an execution. It is prob-ably the fact that capital punishment is accepted as necessary, and yet instinc-tively felt to be wrong, that gives so many descriptions of executions their tragic atmosphere."

—George Orwell,
quoted in The Death Penalty:
A Debate, Ernest van den Haag
and John P. Conrad

Capital punishment, or the death penalty, has been around for thousands of years. In ancient China, criminals were executed for their offenses (by strangulation and decapitation) as were criminals in ancient India and ancient Babylon. Com-moners were executed with an ax in ancient Egypt, while nobles accused of wrongdoing were ordered to commit sui-cide. In ancient Athens, where no prisons existed, death was a common punishment for a range of crimes. The philosopher Socrates, for example, was convicted of heresy and corrupting youth with his teachings. Since he was a citizen, he was sen-tenced to die by drinking hemlock. In A Day in Old Athens, historian William Stearns Davis called this method of death "extremely humane"—especially in comparison to the punish-ments that Athenians doled out to non-citizens.

Romans also made extensive use of capital punishment, executing criminals convicted of crimes such as perjury, making a disturbance in the city at night, or publishing insulting songs. The use of the death penalty for such relatively minor offenses wasn't confined to ancient times. In England up to the eighteenth century, cutting down a tree or stealing an animal could be punished by death, and children as young as seven were hanged by the state.

Many of the world's major religions have approved of, or at least accepted, capital punishment throughout history. Ancient Jewish law condoned execution by stoning, beheading, and throwing criminals from a high rock, among other punishments. Islam accepted capital punishment when administered by a legal court or, as stated in the Koran, "Take not life, which God has made sacred, except by way of justice and law." Hindu scriptures provide examples of justified capital punishment, though the death penalty seems to contradict many Hindu arguments for non-violence. Buddhism is similarly conflicted. It strongly opposes both the taking of life and political involvement. Though Buddhists often verbally speak against the death penalty, "there seems to be limited Buddhist involvement in Southeast Asian countries to death penalty issues," noted Leanne Fiftal Alarid and Hsiao-Ming Wang in a spring 2001 article in *Social Justice*.

Christianity also has had a mixed response to the death penalty. Jesus Christ was a victim of capital punishment, and the first Christian writers agreed, as Pope St. Clement said, "To witness a man's execution, regardless of the justice of his prosecution, is forbidden by the moral law of Christ." Later Christianity moved away from this position. During the Spanish Inquisition, Catholic religious authorities in Spain burned those convicted of heresy at the stake. And, as James J. Megivern wrote in *The Death Penalty: An Historical and Theological Survey*, "While the major Protestant Reformers called for change in many other things, they had no objection to the death penalty as such."

Despite the consensus in favor of the death penalty throughout most of history, there were some calls for reform. Capital punishment was abolished in China between 747 and 759. William the Conqueror, who ruled England in the 1000s, banned the execution of criminals (though he did allow mutilation). In the eleventh century, the Spanish Jewish scholar Moses Maimonides argued for the elimination of the death penalty, saying, "It is better and more satisfactory to acquit a thousand guilty persons than to put a single innocent one to death." And some Protestant sects, such as the Mennonites founded in the 1500s, opposed capital punishment as contrary to Christian teaching.

The modern movement to abolish the death penalty really started, however, with the Enlightenment in the 1700s. Thinkers such as Michel de Montaigne, Voltaire, and Jean-Jacques Rousseau held an optimistic view of human nature. According to Hans Göran Franck in *The Barbaric Punishment*, "They claimed that every criminal could and should be rehabilitated and improved, a view that was incompatible with the death penalty." Italian enlightenment writer Cesare Beccaria had a powerful influence with his book *Of Crimes and Punishments* (1764) and convinced several European monarchs, including those in Russia, Tuscany, and Austria, to abandon the death penalty (though not permanently, in most cases).

Through the 1800s abolition moved forward haltingly but definitely. In 1794, the Commonwealth of Pennsylvania, with its Quaker roots, abandoned the death penalty. In 1863, Venezuela became the first country to abolish the death penalty. The abolition movement stalled during World War I and World War II, but by the mid-1960s, around twenty-five countries had moved toward abolition. In the 1970s, abolition began to be accepted as an international human rights issue by the United Nations (UN) and, especially, by the European Union (EU). The EU Memorandum on the Death Penalty of February 25, 2000, stated, "The European Union is opposed to the death penalty in all cases and has consistently espoused its universal abolition, working towards this goal." Any state that wishes to join the EU must first abolish the death penalty. As a result, a number of central and eastern European countries eager for closer ties with western Europe abolished capital punishment despite the fact that the death penalty remained quite popular with their citizens and politicians.

Outside Europe, one of the most dramatic cases of abolition occurred in South Africa, a nation that had had one of the highest rates of execution in the world. Following the collapse of apartheid and white-minority rule, however, a new constitution was drawn up, and one year later in 1995, the Constitutional Court declared capital punishment illegal. "It is an understatement to say that this rejection of capital punishment was a breach both with the policies of prior regimes in South Africa and with the traditions and expectations of government in sub-Saharan Africa," noted Franklin E. Zimring in *The Contradictions of American Capital Punishment.*

A majority of the world's countries are now considered abolitionist, either because they have formally rejected the death penalty or because they have effectively stopped executions. Many countries, however, still maintain capital punishment. China, for example, is the world's most populous country and is believed to have executed at least four hundred and seventy people in 2007. After China, the other countries responsible for the most executions are, in order, Iran, Pakistan, Iraq, Sudan, and the United States. These nations accounted for more than 90 percent of the world's reported executions. In addition, in some nations such as Indonesia, the use of the death penalty appears to be on the rise. While abolition continues to gain ground, it seems like it will be many years before the death penalty meets its end.

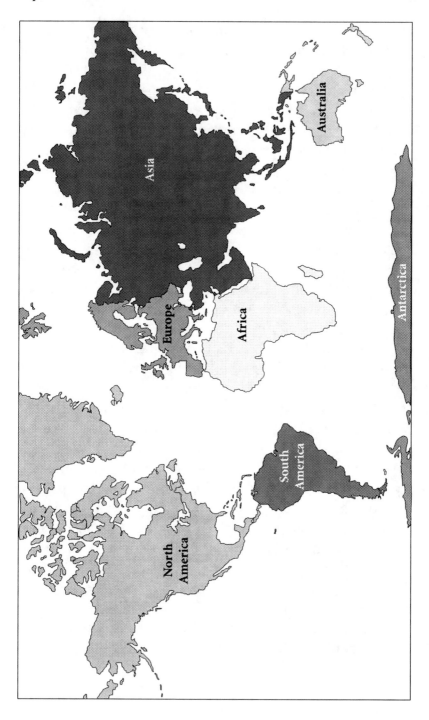

GLOBALVIEWPOINTS

CHAPTER 1

Capital Punishment and Morality

French Juries Should Not Impose the Death Penalty for Even Heinous Crimes

Robert Badinter

Robert Badinter is a French criminal lawyer and politician known for fighting against the death penalty. In this viewpoint, Badinter recounts his final plea to convince a jury not to condemn Patrick Henry, a notorious child murderer, to death. Henry was sentenced to life imprisonment and the verdict was an important milestone in the French abolition of the death penalty.

As you read, consider the following questions:

1. Was Patrick Henry charged with premeditation in the murder of the child?
2. Did Patrick Henry approve of or oppose the death penalty in the cases of Bontems and Buffet?
3. How did the arrival of the riot police foretell the verdict?

Of those moments in Troyes [France], in the courtroom where I pled for Patrick Henry [convicted of kidnapping and murdering a child in 1976], one overriding sensation stays with me: I was defending not only the life of Patrick

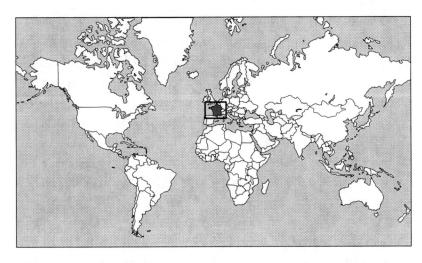

Henry but once again that of Roger Bontems [a criminal who was convicted of complicity in the murder of two prison personnel and was condemned to death despite Badinter's efforts in 1972]. Everything that I hadn't said for him now came streaming out of me for this other man sitting behind me. "The dead clutch onto the living," went an old saying. That day there, in the prisoner's dock behind me, one man transformed into the other. Without a doubt, the prosecutor, by pronouncing the name of Bontems in his submission, had reopened the guilty wound that I had been secretly carrying inside me. And, because he had spoken of him, I would speak of him too.

The Jury Is Responsible for Life or Death

I recalled the guillotine and the ritual of death that went on behind those high prison walls, once that black canopy had been dropped. And, calmly, I explained that if Patrick Henry were to be condemned to death we would go there on that night, to the Santé prison, [the other defense lawyer, Robert] Bocquillon and I, along with Father Clavier. But the prosecutor, he hadn't gone to see Bontems and [Bontems's accomplice, Claude] Buffet die.

I then turned toward the jurors, seeking out their eyes. I didn't want to lose them, not for one second. I told them that from now on, it was just them and him, the jurors and the accused, who were involved in this affair. I said that when the prosecutor asked for the death penalty, he was putting the responsibility of the decision into their hands. There was no chance of the case being overturned because there were no legal grounds for appeal. There wouldn't be any clemency because the president had allowed Christian Ranucci [convicted of the murder of a young girl and executed in 1976] to be executed. So, I told them that it was up to them and them alone to decide whether the young man sitting in the prisoner's dock would live or die. I told them that this was an unparalleled moment in their lives, one that would stay with them for the rest of their days.

They were now watching me with the greatest attention. That is when I truly launched into my plea. I moved forward like a tightrope walker, on a sort of internal wire that kept me above an abyss only I could see. I did what I hadn't thought I would do: I spoke of the facts, quickly, just to sweep aside the accusation of premeditation. I refused to accept the idea that the death of the child had been part of Patrick Henry's plan. And I reminded the jury that the Chambre d'accusation [panel that determines whether enough evidence exists for a case to proceed] hadn't retained that charge against him.

But, even without the premeditation, the murder of the child remained atrocious. And this atrocity inexplicable. Nothing about this young man of twenty-four would have predicted it. Certainly not those petty thefts of his adolescence. "Normal," said the psychiatrists. Was it normal that such a crime had been committed by a "normal" young man of that age? I evoked the limitations of psychiatric knowledge, the uncertainty of the experts. Nobody really knew who this young man was. Not them, the people judging him, not any more than those experts did. But it was they who were being asked to kill him. So, that is what the death penalty was, a judicial sacrifice made amid the shadows of ignorance.

"I told them that from now on, it was just them and him, the jurors and the accused, who were involved in this affair."

The Death Penalty Is Not Justice

I'd arrived at the point I'd wanted to reach from the beginning. . . . I cited the examples of all the European countries, our neighbors, all of them abolitionists. I also reminded the jurors, with even greater vehemence, that it was here in Troyes that Bontems and Buffet had been condemned to death only four years earlier. Patrick Henry had been in the crowd that was screaming "To death!" in front of the courthouse. Had their executions dissuaded him from acting?

I knew that the judges and jurors had already heard these arguments, all these reasons that abolition was justified. But, at this instant, they were listening passionately. It wasn't the fate of the death penalty that was in play, but the life or death of a young man. And it depended on them.

Then, I felt the time had come to evoke that which, at this exceptional moment in their lives, would decide the essential for them. I had arrived at the heart of the matter, at the decision to kill that we had thrust upon them. I reminded them of Nicole Henry [Patrick Henry's sister, who raised him] and his brother, who had both stood sobbing at the witness stand. I asked them where was the justice when the tears of one mother merely echoed the tears of another? I brought out the letter that Madame Ranucci, Christian's mother, had written to Bocquillon. I read it slowly to the jurors:

I am sending you this card so that you can let Patrick Henry's family know I share in their inhuman ordeal. I pray that the life of their son will be spared. I am in agony and I cry like they do when reading or listening to news about the trial where the supporters of the death penalty show proof of their ferocity. They never think that one day their son or their brother might be in the same place. I am the mother of a twenty-two-year-old boy who was condemned to death, Christian Ranucci.

I put down the letter. I was exhausted. I had to conclude. As I stood there at the bar, rising up in me after so many years, I felt the voice of my old mentor, Henry Torrès, and with one ultimate burst of passion I evoked the bishop of Troyes, Monseigneur Fauchet, and the need for forgiveness by those who believe in God. And, for those who only believed in this world, I said I had faith in humanity, that a man was always able to change, to improve himself, to raise himself up to another level. I stopped for an instant. I looked into the eyes of the jurors, one after another. I heard myself say to them: "If you vote as the prosecutor is asking you, I am telling you, time will pass, this tumultuous trial will end and so will the encouragements you've been hearing, and you will be left alone with your decision. The death penalty will be abolished and you will have to live alone with your decision, forever. And your children will one day know you condemned a young man to death. And you will see how they look at you!"

I fell silent. The jurors were still watching me. Several of them were fighting back tears. We remained face-to-face in the silence. I sat down. I could do nothing else for Patrick Henry.

"If you vote as the prosecutor is asking you ... time will pass. ... The death penalty will be abolished and you will have to live alone with your decision, forever."

The Trial Concludes

What happened next surprised us all. Patrick Henry stood up. The presiding judge asked him, as was the law, whether he wished to make a statement. And, to the general amazement,

France Enshrines Death Penalty Abolition in Constitution

Our country [France], has joined the 16 European countries and 45 States in the world which have enshrined the abolition of the death penalty in their fundamental texts. Indeed, article 66-1 of the [French] Constitution, in Title VIII on the judicial authority, now states, "No one can be sentenced to the death penalty".

M. Pascal Clément,
"Pascal Clément on Permanent, Total
Abolition of Capital Punishment in France,"
France in the United Kingdom Online,
March 28, 2007. www.ambafrance-uk.org.

he spoke. His voice, as it came across the microphone, lost the coldness, the distant quality that had made him appear so odious at times. It was at last him, this young man, who was expressing himself because, without a doubt, this was the last chance for him to tell us the truth before he was taken away into the night. He was calm, but at the same time very emotional. "I am going to try," he began. "I've never been able to open up. I've always kept everything inside me." He said that if he'd cried, he would have been seen as a coward. That, since he couldn't cry, everyone looked at him like a monster. He added that the hours and the months that had passed had given him the chance to reflect. He knew what he had done was horrible. He knew it better than anybody else. For a brief instant, he stopped himself. He was ashen and short of breath. And, finally, he said those words we were all waiting to hear, they now spilled from his mouth: "I regret this from the bottom of my heart. For a long time, I wanted to ask Philippe's parents for forgiveness. I wanted to tell them how horrified I am by what I did and how I suffer because there is nothing I can do to fix it." Then, abruptly, he gasped, "I can't go on," and he pushed away the microphone.

Everything had been said. The judges and the jurors retired to deliberate. Patrick Henry was escorted out by guards. The courtroom, paralyzed during the final submissions, came back to life. The spectators dispersed. Small groups formed, conversations hummed, a few went out into the atrium. I stayed in my place for a moment, exchanging several words with [Badinter's assistant, François] Binet. He said he was confident. I refused all hope—or more aptly, I thought, all illusions. Several lawyers from our office had come to sit in on the day's session, out of curiosity and also to share the burden of the ordeal. They all appeared to be moved, and their faces and their words shone with friendship. But I had known too many judicial battles to share the optimism they were showing. Frédéric Pottecher, one of the renowned legal journalists, came to tell me in his gruff manner that I had done a good job. I replied: "They're going to condemn him to death anyway." It was, to begin with, a means of conjuring away bad luck by not appearing overconfident. But, deep inside myself, I was expecting nothing other than to have to take that same road I'd already traveled, to return to the Santé prison to visit Patrick Henry each morning in his death row cell.

Elisabeth [Badinter's wife] had joined me. Her expression was troubled. I couldn't bear to be in the courtroom any longer. We left, we found Bocquillon. He was grey with anxiety. I told him how much I had liked his submission. He scoffed, "You're making fun of me! I told them a load of nonsense." I left him, took off my robes, and descended the stairs to the basement cells where the accused was kept during breaks in the trial. There I found Patrick Henry. I sat down close to him, just as I had sat close to Bontems not so long ago. He thanked me, almost warmly. I told him how important it was for Philippe's parents, and also for himself, that he had finally asked for their forgiveness. But would they be able to forgive him, he who had killed their child? We exchanged a few more words. I could feel the same anguish swell inside me that had so tormented me before my final plea. I left him and climbed back up to the atrium, to the voices, to life.

The atrium was teeming with people. I went out onto the courthouse steps with Binet and stood in the glacial air. Night had fallen. Behind the police barricades, several hundred people had gathered. I knew all too well what they were waiting for. I returned to the courtroom.

The Jury Returns

The wait wasn't long. I saw Binet coming toward me, obviously flustered. He pulled me aside, whispering: "The riot police have arrived." I was stunned. I had told him that in the event the verdict wasn't death, the presiding judge would surely call for police reinforcements to contain the explosion of fury. I now heard the sound of the police trucks or vans pulling into their places beneath the windows and in the courtyard. At almost the same moment, the court bell rang out. Everyone retook their places amid the chaos. I looked at the clock: The deliberation had lasted one and a half hours. The judges and the jurors reentered the courtroom. I watched them intently. When Patrick Henry arrived at the prisoner's dock, I saw the eyes of several jurors converge upon him. Yet, when Bontems had been condemned to death, I'd noted that not a single juror had turned their eyes toward the prisoner's dock when the decision was read out. They had all stared out ahead of them, at some invisible horizon, as if death could not be looked in the face.

The presiding judge began to read the decision. He went quickly. To the questions regarding the guilt of the accused, the answers could only be "Yes, with a majority of votes." It was only the last question that was important. The presiding judge paused almost imperceptibly. "Did there exist any extenuating circumstances that favored the accused?—YES."

"Though he hadn't been condemned to death, Patrick Henry had nonetheless lost his life."

In the uproar that followed, we could barely make out the words "imprisoned for life." We heard a scream: It was Patrick Henry's mother. As for him, he had brought his hand to his lips. He looked bewildered. The spectators were on their feet. The presiding judge called the courtroom to order, and added: "Patrick Henry, the court has shown you tremendous goodwill. You must not let it down. We are counting on you." Patrick Henry whispered: "I thank you all. You won't regret this." I let myself fall back into my seat. I was empty. All I knew was that I wouldn't be returning to that cell on death row.

Journalists were running to the telephones to report the news. Outside, the shouting grew louder: "Death to the murderer! Justice is rotten!" Patrick leaned out to kiss his mother, his sister, his brother—all standing next to the dock. He shook hands with Mademoiselle Gérard, the investigating judge, who was visibly moved by the events. Bocquillon was exultant. He embraced me. He hugged Patrick Henry as the guards were leading him away. He would live. His future had been reduced to nothing more than prison walls. He already belonged to the prison universe. We knew that "life" didn't actually exist in the criminal code. But how many decades would slip by before he could even begin to hope of receiving parole? The child was dead. Though he hadn't been condemned to death, Patrick Henry had nonetheless lost his life.

Europe Is Hypocritical to Oppose the Death Penalty but Not Abortion

John Jalsevac

John Jalsevac writes regularly for LifeSiteNews.com. In this view-point, he argues that European nations priding themselves on death penalty abolition need to promote life in other areas as well. Specifically, he argues that the Polish government and Pope Benedict are both correct to suggest that Europe should oppose euthanasia and abortion. Europe's World Day Against the Death Penalty is hollow, Jalsevac maintains. Instead, he thinks that a day for the sanctity of all human life is needed.

As you read, consider the following questions:

1. Does Pope Benedict support or oppose capital punishment?
2. Who is Robert Latimer?
3. According to John Jalsevac, why did Poland feel a World Day Against the Death Penalty in Europe wasn't all that productive?

Featured prominently on the homepage of the not-so-subtly titled prodeathpenalty.com is a quotation by a Mr. John McAdams, a professor at Marquette University. He quips, "If

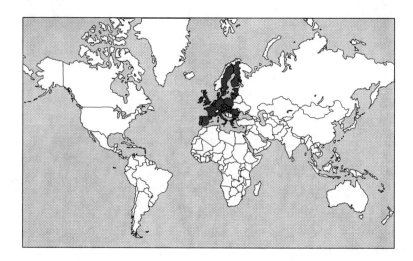

we execute murderers and there is in fact no deterrent effect, we have killed a bunch of murderers. If we fail to execute murderers, and doing so would in fact have deterred other murders, we have allowed the killing of a bunch of innocent victims. I would much rather risk the former. This, to me, is not a tough call."

To Mr. McAdams it might not be a tough call, and to most of history this was not a tough call, but to most of the Western world, it is.

Indeed, so far the EU has completely eradicated the death penalty within its borders; so too has England, and so too have Canada and Mexico; and even in the U.S., for all of its reputation for out-dated cowboy-style justice, capital punishment has become an endangered species, nearly drowned out of existence by a flood of red-tape. For that matter, even the Catholic Church, that great champion of the union of stake, flame, and heretic, has in recent decades taken the lead in the effort to bring an end to capital punishment. (Of course, the Church has never actually condemned the death penalty as intrinsically immoral, but only "imprudent" and "unnecessary" in the developed world's socio-political environment. But who has time for theological distinctions like that?)

This is not an article in defense of the death penalty. Indeed, it was only a month ago when I participated in a parliamentary-style debate in which I argued so vociferously, and (so I thought) so convincingly against the use of the death penalty that I actually began to believe I might have been right. It isn't the death penalty that's the issue here, but hypocrisy and muddle-headedness.

Yesterday, Pope Benedict, in his annual address to the diplomatic corps, touched on capital punishment, giving the EU a pat on the back for its abolitionist efforts. His statement, however, calls to mind the old saying about a "dagger in a smile."

"It isn't the death penalty that's the issue here, but hypocrisy and muddle-headedness."

"I rejoice that on 18 December the General Assembly of the United Nations adopted a resolution calling upon States to institute a moratorium on the use of the death penalty," said the Pope, at which point I presume the EU representatives smiled appreciatively and murmured their congratulations to each other. They also probably completely missed the second half of the sentence, which was the good part with the stab at the EU's hypocrisy: "And I earnestly hope that this initiative will lead to public debate on the sacred character of human life."

The post-Christian West is a funny thing. For all of its efforts to abolish morality and any notion of sin from the public square, it just can't seem to shake that medieval notion of an objective right and wrong. The best it can seem to do is get all muddle-headed about what right and wrong are.

For instance, there's a lot of chatter in "progressive" papers and parliaments these days about making it legal for a doctor to prescribe barbiturates to a "patient", so that he knock himself off. As I understand it, this is supposed to be the newest addition to the ever growing catalogue of human rights. But at the same time, in the very same papers and parliaments, there is a very successful movement working to completely outlaw smoking, "because smoking kills." The understood implication is that killing yourself is wrong; but I'm not sure how that jives with this newfound human right to down a fatal dose of barbiturates. While I'm no fan of cigarettes (I'm more of a pipe and cigar guy myself), show me a cigarette and a syringe of barbiturates and I'll take the cigarette over the drugs any day of the week, because I know which one kills.

Fact is, for all of our talk about the right to life and human dignity, in the West we're all about killing these days. We're all about killing ourselves: and, judging by the widespread show of support for men like Canada's Robert Latimer, who murdered his handicapped daughter out of "mercy", it's becoming increasingly fashionable to kill other people.

"Fact is, for all of our talk about the right to life and human dignity, in the West we're all about killing these days."

Then, of course, there's the refuse of abortion—the millions of fetuses annually that are chopped up and tossed in the Dumpster for the landfill. I know. I know that the fetus is supposed to not be a human person, and therefore everything's kosher. But this is just another example of the sort of muddle-headedness I'm talking about. Greenpeace and the World Wildlife Fund would have us treat our pet hamsters more humanely than we treat our unborn children, human or not. Even if we choose not to define the fetus as human, it's certainly a living creature; so it seems that the least we can do is treat it as decently as we treat other living creatures. But I've seen no "save the fetuses" campaign from Greenpeace, the WWF, or any other animal rights groups.

For Catholic Church, Abortion Is More Important than the Death Penalty

Not all moral issues have the same moral weight as abortion and euthanasia. For example, if a Catholic were to be at odds with the Holy Father on the application of capital punishment or on the decision to wage war, he would not for that reason be considered unworthy to present himself to receive Holy Communion. While the Church exhorts civil authorities to seek peace, not war, and to exercise discretion and mercy in imposing punishment on criminals, it may still be permissible to take up arms to repel an aggressor or to have recourse to capital punishment. There may be a legitimate diversity of opinion even among Catholics about waging war and applying the death penalty, but not, however, with regard to abortion and euthanasia.

Joseph Ratzinger,
"Worthiness to Receive Communion—General Principles,"
Catholic Culture Online, 2004. *www.catholicculture.org.*

John McAdams defends the death penalty because he believes that it will save innocent lives; his mistake, however, is to think that the West cares any more for innocent lives than it does for the guilty. Sometimes, in fact, things seem quite the opposite—that we're in favor of killing all sorts of people, just so long as they're innocent.

In the West life is a right, and life is sacred, just as long as the life we're talking about is guilty of a capital crime, or incapable of either innocence or guilt (your pet hamster). That is the message being broadcasted to the world by the West's obsession with abolishing the death penalty, and its simultaneous insistence on vociferously protecting and championing abortion, assisted suicide and euthanasia.

This is quite the paradox. It is also the paradox that Poland dared to protest back in September when the EU was proposing a World Day Against the Death Penalty. The Polish government called down upon itself all sorts of outrage when it suggested that perhaps a World Day Against the Death Penalty wasn't all that productive, since the EU had already outlawed capital punishment, but that a world day dedicated to the sanctity of all human life could do a great deal of good.

". . .we're in favor of killing all sorts of people, just so long as they're innocent."

"We think that when anybody wants to discuss a problem of death in the context of the law it is also worth to discuss on euthanasia and abortion in this context," said a spokesman for the Polish delegation.

"I think it is hypocritical on the part of the EU to promote abortion, destructive lifestyles and euthanasia and at the same time to pretend to care about the right to life in only one case—death penalty," concurred Krzysztof Bosak, of the League of Polish Right (LPR), who is also a member of the Council of Europe's Parliamentary Assembly.

And so for months on end Poland endured being labeled medieval, and backwards, and reactionary and bloodthirsty. The World Day Against the Death Penalty was passed when the new Polish government came into power, allowing the liberal media and politicians to feel warm and fuzzy inside for having fought so hard to protect the right to life and human dignity.

Pope Benedict, however, yesterday reminded the EU that they have not gone far enough—not nearly far enough. It is good, he suggested, that the EU recognizes that human beings have dignity, and that it protects that dignity by abolishing the death penalty. But even still, he added, the former Polish government was perfectly right. A World Day Against the Death

Penalty makes no sense without a world day for the sanctity of all human life. We all look forward to the day when the EU, and every nation across the world, will recognize such a day.

Thailand's Death Penalty Contradicts Buddhist Morality

Danthong Breen

Danthong Breen is the chairman of the Union of Civil Liberties in Thailand. In this viewpoint, he discusses seminars on the death penalty in Thailand, which religious leaders of various faiths attended. Buddhist attendees explained that Buddhism opposes all killing. Breen sees this position as in accordance with a growing international consensus against the death penalty. Muslim leaders at the seminars noted that Islam accepts the death penalty, but also puts a high value on mercy. Christian leaders noted that Christianity generally opposes the death penalty. Breen concludes that religious teachings reject the death penalty.

As you read, consider the following questions:

1. At the time of the drafting of the Universal Declaration of Human Rights, how many nations had abolished the death penalty?
2. Are Muslims the majority in Thailand?
3. What does Danthong Breen say is the highest authority on Earth?

"Buddhism considers it wrong to kill even a mosquito, so how can we accept that it is right to execute a human being?" These words were part of an uncompromising rejec-

Danthong Breen, "The Death Penalty: Religious Perspectives," *Bangkok Post Online*, October 1, 2008. Copyright © 1996–2008 The Post Publishing Public Company Limited. Reproduced by permission.

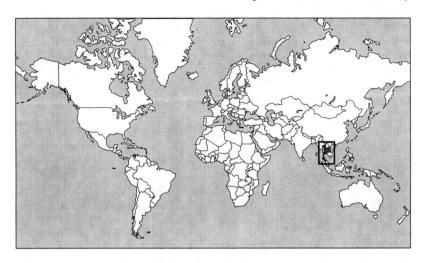

tion of capital punishment addressed to a recent gathering at Wat Suan Dok in Chiang Mai, by a senior monk. He enlarged on the theme in even stronger words: "According to the teachings of the Buddha, every living being has a right to life; even to think of harming any creature is a mistake."

He explained that in Buddhist thinking, harmful thoughts lead to bad speech, and hence to bad action. It is impossible to prevent harmful thoughts from resulting in crime. The inevitable outcome of crime from bad thoughts cannot be prevented by fear of death. But shame can disable the harmful intention, change thought and develop a human being. Every prisoner can change his nature, to become pure.

Seminars Examine Religious Perspectives on the Death Penalty

In recent months, seminars have been taking place in several locations throughout Thailand to examine religious perspectives on the death penalty. Three seminars were devoted to a Buddhist perspective: in Chiang Mai, Ubon Ratchathani and Ayutthaya provinces, with a total audience of up to 150 monks. A seminar at a Muslim centre considered capital punishment from a Muslim perspective. Finally, the perspectives of Buddhism, Islam and Christianity were presented together at a seminar held at the Office of the National Human Rights Commission in Bangkok.

This year [2008] marks the 60th anniversary of the Universal Declaration of Human Rights, the agreed formulation of basic human rights held by all members of the United Nations. There are 30 articles to the Declaration and the foundation of all other rights is that stated in Article 3: "Everyone has the right to life."

These six simple words rejected the monstrous murder of innocents known as the Holocaust, but extended to all killing everywhere, and at every time. When the Declaration was being composed there were some who wished to include an exception to justify judicial execution, but after months of debate, the instinct to prohibit all killing prevailed.

The [World War II] war trials at Nuremberg, which established for the first time in history the category of crimes against humanity, had just ended with the execution of 10 of the defendants. It was as if accounts had to be settled before anger and the need for vengeance could be exhausted. The six words had to wait for future generations to fulfil their promise.

At the time when the Universal Declaration was drafted, only eight countries in the world had renounced the death penalty. Today, that number has grown to 133. From the rate of growth in recent years in the number of abolitionist countries, one can estimate the day and hour when the barbaric practice of judicial execution is likely to go the way of slavery and end forever.

On Dec. 18, 2007 the General Assembly of the United Nations again took up the issue of the right to life and, by a majority vote of 104 to 54, declared in favour of a Moratorium on the Death Penalty. The motion was bitterly opposed by some member countries, and the decision is not mandatory. But a majority vote of the General Assembly carries immense authority. At the least, all members of the UN are mandated to consider their practice of the death penalty and to take account of a world opinion that increasingly favours abolition.

Thailand was one of the minority countries opposing the Moratorium. The Thai delegate had earlier explained his stance by asserting that there are worthless people who do not deserve to live! His sentiment cannot be justified by the religious beliefs of the people of Thailand.

The monk in Chiang Mai continued his discourse. "Execution is a legal crime that is not different from illegal crime. A judge who orders execution by word or document is also guilty according to Buddhism. There is no exception."

"All religions value the life of the individual, and affirm the human potential for reform of a wrongdoer."

Religions Struggle with the Death Penalty

The seminars have been organised by the Union for Civil Liberty in cooperation with the National Human Rights Commission, with funding provided by the European Union, the Netherlands and France.

The death penalty is an issue of ethics and morality, areas of primary interest in religion and in the humanism which goes hand in hand with religion. Religions have grappled with the issue of the death penalty throughout their history. All religions value the life of the individual, and affirm the human potential for reform of a wrongdoer. On the part of the injured, they teach mercy and forgiveness as the only exit from pain and the wrong done. It is perhaps only in China, which carries out 80 percent of all executions in the world that the condemned person is considered a pest to be eliminated as expeditiously as possible.

Traditionally, religions have lived with the death penalty by separating themselves from actual executions. Buddhist

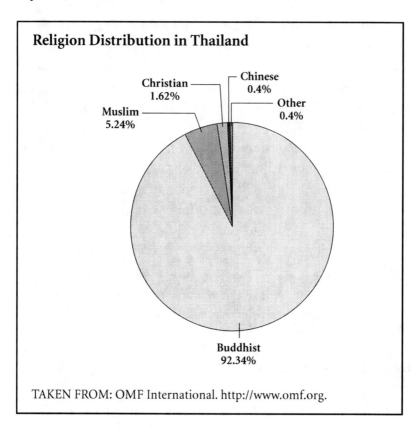

Religion Distribution in Thailand

Christian 1.62%

Chinese 0.4%

Other 0.4%

Muslim 5.24%

Buddhist 92.34%

TAKEN FROM: OMF International. http://www.omf.org.

monks attending the seminars who accept the death penalty, defined their objective as teaching people how to be good. Those who listen to the teaching do not incur the death penalty. If they ignore the teaching and commit serious crime then the death penalty is their fate.

There was an old rule in the monkhood that a monk must make a detour to avoid walking through a place where executions were carried out, emphasizing the separation of monks from justified secular punishment. A similar practice in the past allowed Christian courts to find a person guilty of a capital crime, but the condemned criminal had to be handed over to secular authority to be executed. Can guilt be so delegated? And what if an innocent person is condemned—with whom does responsibility lie?

Muslim Perspectives on the Death Penalty

From an Islamic perspective, the death penalty for certain crimes is commanded by Allah, as recorded in the Koran. At first sight this might appear an end to the discussion. But Islam is a highly developed and nuanced religion. Muslim speakers emphasised that Islam is part of the human heritage belonging to the whole human race, not just to Muslims. It contains an immense font of wisdom.

The full expression of Muslim law, Sharia, is found only in a majority Muslim society where peace and security reign. The first condition of judgement is a strict requirement of evidence which all but eliminates the possibility of wrongful conviction. The defining quality of Allah is that he is merciful. Repentance and the forgiveness of the wrongdoer are always possible. Even as an executioner raises a sword to carry out sentence, he looks to the relatives of the victim. If they give a sign that they accept repentance and offer forgiveness the sentence of death is suspended, to be substituted for by restitution and a lesser penalty. Allah will reward them for their gesture of mercy.

A story is told from the life of Prophet Muhammad where he tried again and again to extend pardon to a woman who had committed adultery but who herself insisted on execution. The Prophet continued to question her executioners, fearing that they had perhaps ignored some sign of repentance.

"From an Islamic perspective, the death penalty for certain crimes is commanded by Allah, as recorded in the Koran."

However, there is a contrast between practice in a Muslim state where peace and prosperity reign, and the imperfect situation elsewhere. In Thailand, Muslims are a minority who obey and respect the law of the country. But recognising the shortcomings of a prevailing imperfect system of justice, they are ready to agree that a suspension of the death penalty is to be preferred.

There is much to be learned from the value placed by Islam on forgiveness, which aims to undo the harm due to wrongdoing. In several cultures, a crime is seen not just as the harm done by one individual to another, but as a harm which involves a community. Can the death penalty heal a community? Can it reconstruct damaged relationships? Can it bring back those whose lives were lost? On the contrary, if forgiveness is extended to a culprit who genuinely repents, a community can implement "correction," not just in the sense of punishment, but in working to make things right.

"A speaker on the Christian perspective towards the death penalty recalled the unique experience of Christianity whose founder was condemned and executed."

Christian Perspectives on the Death Penalty

A speaker on the Christian perspective towards the death penalty recalled the unique experience of Christianity whose founder was condemned and executed. Based on this memory, Christians strongly rejected the death penalty in the first 400 years. They accepted the death penalty as part of Roman law, only when they were given citizenship in the Roman state. Many centuries passed before the majority of Christians could return to their first belief.

Today, the majority of Christians strongly oppose the death penalty and support the movement for abolition. A long and tortuous history of progressing from an acceptance of the death penalty to its rejection, in spite of the clear example and teaching of their founder, illustrates the difficulty in changing perception and waking to the implications of religious belief.

Religious Teachings Reject the Death Penalty

The seminars have strongly presented to religious believers in Thailand the dilemma of holding to beliefs on the unique value of human life, on the primacy of mercy and forgiveness, and at the same time assenting to the taking of life in their name by a process of justice rejected by the highest authority on Earth, the UN General Assembly.

It is time to weigh the arguments which suggest that the death penalty is not a solution to crime, that it does not deter more than the punishment of long imprisonment, and that the life of any human being has a value which cannot be taken away.

The Morality of the Death Penalty in India Is Unclear

Vir Sanghvi

Vir Sanghvi is an Indian editor and television celebrity. He is the editorial director of the Hindustan Times. *In the following viewpoint, Sanghvi admits that he is unsure whether convicted terrorist Mohammad Afzal should be hanged. He notes that the death penalty does not deter and that the execution may even inspire more terrorist acts of revenge. He also argues, however, that Indian police violence kills far more people than executions do and that holding terrorists in prison indefinitely can encourage terrorist acts in an effort to free them.*

As you read, consider the following questions:

1. What convinced Vir Sanghvi that holding terrorists in prison might encourage hijackings and other terrorist violence?
2. Were all of those accused of complicity in the attacks on Parliament with Mohammad Afzal convicted?
3. Does Sanghvi believe that the U.S. invasion of Iraq reduced or increased the number of terrorists?

Should Mohammed Afzal [convicted of conspiring to attack the Indian Parliament building in 2001] be hanged? The

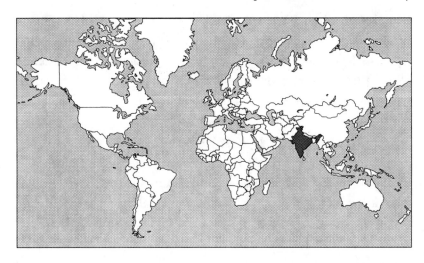

honest answer is: I do not know. I have wrestled long and hard with the question and I still cannot decide what the right thing to do would be.

My problems with the sentence begin with my doubts about the death penalty itself. For much of my youth, I accepted the traditional liberal arguments against capital punishment.

Capital Punishment Does Not Deter

And those arguments are intellectually unassailable. The basis of all punishment is deterrence. We do not put a man in jail only to get him out of the way (if that were so, then we would never release him); we do it to make an example out of him, to tell people that they will also be punished if they break the law.

There are arguments about what constitutes effective deterrence. For instance, Singapore believes that very strict punishments are required to deter criminals. Many Arab countries believe that, for true deterrence, punishments should be publicly carried out. And European countries think they can get by with lenient punishments. But nobody disputes that the point of putting somebody in jail, of hanging him or of flogging him in public is to deter others.

The problem with the death penalty is that it has absolutely no deterrent value. In every society, where capital punishment has been abolished, there has either been no effect at all on the crime rate or—and this is the significant bit—there have actually been fewer murders after they stopped hanging people.

Consequently, nearly every developed country (with the exception of some American states—but then, development is a relative term) has abolished capital punishment. They regard it as a barbaric hangover from a medieval era where punishment was about revenge and bloodlust. And none of them has suffered as a result of the abolition.

"More people are killed by policemen on the streets of India in an average week than are hanged after due process in a decade."

Some Reasons Not to Oppose Capital Punishment

As convincing as all this is, I have become an agnostic [one who is doubtful about something] on the subject of the death penalty in India: I am no longer as passionate about demanding its abolition. There are two reasons for this. The first is that the death penalty is handed out every day on the streets of India by policemen and paramilitary troops in the form of the so-called encounter [extrajudicial killings in which police shoot alleged gangsters or terrorists in gun battles]. Given that there is widespread public support for such encounters, and that they seem set to continue, does it make any sense to get so self-righteous about a few hangings?

As weak as the case for capital punishment may be, a hanging is, at least, the result of due process where a judge looks at the evidence and a defendant is given a right to present his case. On the other hand, encounters follow no process, there is no sense of justice and innocent people are frequently bumped off. Moreover, the numbers tell their own story. More people are killed by policemen on the streets of India in an average week than are hanged after due process in a decade. So, if you really want to get agitated about the right to life, then don't recycle a largely irrelevant Western debate about hanging; focus on encounters instead.

There is a second reason why I am less passionate about opposing hanging. After IC-814 [Indian Airlines Flight 814, hijacked by Pakistani terrorists in 1999], I am now convinced that the longer we keep terrorists in jail, the greater is the incentive for their compatriots to hijack planes or to seize hostages to secure their release. In this case, the death penalty is a deterrent. It is the jail sentence that will encourage more terrorists.

Arguments About Afzal Case Are Overly Polarised

Nevertheless, I do not pretend that my arguments can undermine the intellectual basis of the case against capital punishment. And those who support hanging in India usually fall back on two rather tiresome and well-worn strategies. Either they make the case for revenge ("Shouldn't we avenge the guard who was murdered by this terrorist?" etc.) or they play to cheap sentiment ("What will we tell the father of this murdered girl who has spent his life fighting for justice?"). Both arguments may have emotional power, but they have zero intellectual merit.

Which brings us to the case of Mohammed Afzal. The most distressing aspect of the campaigns for and against his hanging is how communally polarised the debate has become. The people who demand that he be killed forthwith tend to be sangh parivar [an Indian nationalist movement] sympathisers. Equally, many of those who ask that his sentence be commuted play the minority card. Some Kashmiri politicians

Class Bias in India's Death Penalty System

The randomness of the lethal lottery that is the death penalty in India is perhaps not so random. It goes without saying that the less wealth and influence a person has, the more likely ... [he or she is] to be sentenced to death. ... The Supreme Court itself has acknowledged the class bias in death sentences. ... Justice [P.N.] Bhagwati [in a dissenting opinion] commented, "Death penalty has a certain class complexion or class bias inasmuch as it is largely the poor and the down-trodden who are the victims of this extreme penalty. We would hardly find a rich or affluent person going to the gallows." The judge concluded: "There can be no doubt that the death penalty in its actual operation is discriminatory, for it strikes mostly against the poor and deprived section of the community ... this circumstance also adds to the arbitrary and capricious nature of the death penalty and renders it unconstitutional."

*Amnesty International India
and People's Union for Civil Liberty,
"Lethal Lottery: The Death Penalty in India,"*
Amnesty International Online,
May 2008. www.amnesty.org.

have already begun to portray him as a martyr put to death by heartless Hindu policemen. The sub-text to all this is that it will now be almost impossible for a Muslim President [A.P.J. Abdul Kalam] to grant him clemency. Which is sad and against the principles of Indian secularism.

As for the case against hanging him, I have to say that I am not convinced. It is all very well to argue that the police are biased, that they torture suspects and that they manufacture evidence: In our hearts, we already know all that. But it is quite another thing to say that Afzal's trial was unfair or that the judge was biased. Let's not forget that others accused of complicity in the same attack were acquitted. If the judge was biased, he would have hanged everybody. And let's also remember that it wasn't just a single judge who found him guilty. His appeals were also turned down.

Nor does it make any sense to say that the poor fellow wasn't physically present in Parliament when it was attacked and is therefore only a minor conspirator. This is the equivalent of saying that you can't really blame Osama bin Laden for the 9/11 [terrorist] attacks because he did not fly one of the planes. In cases of terrorism, physical presence is not a necessary condition for guilt.

I am almost as annoyed by the Kashmiri arguments against his hanging. As far as I can tell, the basic appeal is as follows: He may well have attacked Parliament but, on the other hand, he could equally have been framed. Besides, he is a Kashmiri so we think you should commute his sentence.

This is nonsense. The man has been convicted by a court [of] law. It doesn't matter if he's a Hindu or a Muslim, a Bihari or a Kashmiri; as far as we are concerned, he's an Indian. I find it particularly shameful that so many mainstream political parties in the Valley have tried to whip up sentiment against the sentence by playing on subliminal communal fears.

Some Anti-Death Penalty Arguments Make Sense

But two arguments against the hanging seem to have some merit. The first is that many of those who got off in the Parliament attack case had heavyweight legal representation. Afzal, on the other hand, had no access to top lawyers, and relied on an amicus curiae [a friend of the court]. The sad reality of the Indian legal system is that even if you massacre a family in the middle of Connaught Place [a vibrant business district in

Delhi] or Flora Fountain [a famous ornamental fountain in Mumbai] in front of hundreds of witnesses, you'll probably be found innocent if you get somebody like Ram Jethmalani [a famous criminal lawyer and politician] to defend you or have enough money to buy off the witnesses. I always find it particularly distressing that the overwhelming majority of those hanged are poor people with no access to fancy legal brains. You could argue that Afzal belongs in this category.

But it is the second argument that still troubles me. Why are we punishing Afzal? Is it to deter other terrorists? If so, then I'm not sure that it's going to work.

Look at it this way: Suppose we do hang him, what do you suppose the consequences will be? Of course, we will deter terrorists from hijacking planes to free him. But given how high passions in the Valley are now running, isn't there a danger that we will turn him into a martyr? That extremists and fundamentalists will use his execution as an emotional plea for recruitment?

"I always find it particularly distressing that the overwhelming majority of those hanged are poor people with no access to fancy legal brains."

Let's take a parallel. When the US went into Iraq, conservative policy wonks argued that the introduction of democracy into Iraq would enable the Arab world to see a liberal society up-close. And once the Arabs discovered the virtues of democracy, they would discard religious fundamentalism and feudalism.

In fact, the invasion had exactly the opposite effect. Fundamentalists were able to portray it as part of a Western war against Islam and used it as part of their recruitment drive. Eventually, the invasion of Iraq created more terrorists than al Qaeda could ever have hoped for.

Is this too far-fetched a comparison? Is it wrong to suggest that the hanging of a Kashmiri at a time when passions have been stirred up may well serve as a rallying point for extremists and help them convert more youth to their cause? That, far from being a deterrent, it could actually serve as an encouragement?

There Is No Easy Answer to the Death Penalty

I'm not sure. And I also recognise the danger of accepting the 'public opinion' argument when it comes to handing out justice.

A basic tenet of a liberal society is that justice is not subject to swings in the public mood but is absolute.

All of which takes us back to where I started: Should Afzal be hanged? I still don't know. The issues are too complex for there to be any one right or wrong answer. Each of us will have to rely on our conscience and judgment to reach a view that is fair and just. And one that is pragmatic.

Judaism Supports the Death Penalty

Steven Plaut

Steven Plaut is a professor at the Graduate School of Business Administration at the University of Haifa and is a columnist for The Jewish Press. *In this viewpoint, he argues that Jewish liberals are wrong to oppose capital punishment. Plaut argues that the Bible advocates capital punishment as a way of preserving human dignity. He adds that Israel should impose the death penalty on terrorists even if it does not deter because the death penalty makes the moral statement that killing innocents is unacceptable.*

As you read, consider the following questions:

1. According to Steven Plaut, why does the Bible say that especially vile murderers should not be executed?
2. According to Plaut, who was the lone person executed in Israel?
3. According to Plaut, what role do juries play in the Israeli legal system?

One of the most popular causes among Jewish liberals is opposition to capital punishment. The Religious Action Center, the political SWAT Team of the Reform movement, has long considered opposing capital punishment to be one of its highest priorities. Many other groups of Jewish liberals, and some non-liberals, oppose all forms of capital punishment, supposedly in the name of Jewish ethics and the invariably misrepresented *tikkun olam* [a Hebrew phrase meaning "repairing the world"].

Whenever one comes out in favor of capital punishment, one inevitably hears shrieks from such folks about how execution is inhumane, how it violates human dignity, how every human soul, even that of murderers, has been created in God's image and so should be preserved at all costs.

The Bible Supports Capital Punishment

This is all very interesting. There's just one little problem, though. The Bible makes it crystal clear that the way one acknowledges that human souls are created in God's image and deserving of respect and dignity is through capital punishment. Just read Genesis 9:6: "A man who spills human blood, his own blood shall be spilled by man because God made man in His own Image." Not just among Jews, by the way, but among all sons of Noah.

In other words, the preservation of human dignity requires capital punishment of convicted murderers. The position of Judaism is the opposite of the position espoused by liberals. It is precisely because of man's creation in God's image that capital punishment is declared justified and necessary. Human dignity requires execution of murderers, not compassion for their souls.

Moreover, capital punishment is regarded by Judaism as a favor for the capital sinner, a form of atonement and redemption. Ordinary murderers are allowed to achieve atonement for their souls in their execution. Only especially vile murderers—such as a false witness whose lies are discovered after the person who was framed has been executed, or a man who sacrifices both his son and his daughter to the pagan god Molokh—are denied execution because they are regarded as beyond redemption through capital punishment. Again, execution preserves human dignity, it does not defile it.

Israelis have for years debated the pros and cons of capital punishment for convicted terrorist murderers. Up to this point, Israel has never had a death penalty, the lone exception being the execution of the Nazi beast ["architect of the Holocaust" Adolf] Eichmann. Naturally, the Beautiful Left is vehemently opposed to the very idea of capital punishment.

So maybe the time is right to take a deep breath and step back and reexamine the issue. Should Israel have a death penalty?

"... *the preservation of human dignity requires capital punishment of convicted murderers.*"

Capital Punishment Makes a Moral Statement

Opponents of the death penalty say it does not deter terrorism or violence. But how do they know? How do they know the level of violent crime the United States would experience if it did not have a death penalty—or if it had a more widely applied one? How do they know whether the level of terrorism would decrease in an Israel with a death penalty compared to an Israel without one?

Actually, the death penalty should be implemented against terrorists even if it doesn't deter terrorism. It should be implemented because it represents a great moral statement. It is the moral and ethical thing to do. Executing terrorists makes a statement that they are scum with no claim [to] a right to life. Capital punishment represents a moral and just vengeance. It represents a declaration of good and evil. We do not build statues of heroes and otherwise honor them because we necessarily believe these are utilitarian and will lead to the emergence of new heroes, but rather because we are making a

Israel: Deaths in Suicide Terrorist Attacks, 2000–2007

Year	Deaths
2000	0
2001	85
2002	220
2003	142
2004	55
2005	22
2006	15
2007	3

TAKEN FROM: Israel: Ministry of Foreign Affairs, "Suicide and Other Bombing Attacks in Israel Since the Declaration of Principles (Sept. 1993)," 2008. www.mfa.gov.il.

statement as a society regarding our values and what we honor. Executing terrorists is precisely the same sort of societal statement, in the opposite direction.

It is for this moral reason that traditional Judaism unambiguously endorses the death penalty for premeditated murder. It does not do so because of any sociological speculation about the powers of deterrence, and it is clear that the death penalty is viewed as a just punishment even if it deters nothing at all.

". . .the death penalty should be implemented against terrorists even if it doesn't deter terrorism. . .because it represents a great moral statement."

Opponents of the Death Penalty Are Wrong

Opponents of the death penalty argue that implementing it would represent capitulating [giving in] to the populist demands and pressures of the public. Huh? That is essentially a concession that the general electorate favors it and so its establishment would be the democratic thing to do. Denying the death penalty is elitist and anti-democratic.

Opponents of the death penalty in Israel argue that Arab terrorists would retaliate by mistreating or killing Jews they capture. One does not know whether to laugh or to cry at this claim. The PLO [Palestine Liberation Organization] and its sister organizations already lynch, torture and murder every Jew they can lay their hands on, including children—all this while Israel has no death penalty. So what exactly is there to lose?

Opponents argue that it would be dehumanizing to ask an Israeli to act as an executioner, as the one who would push the button or pull the switch. They worry it would be hard to find someone to play the executioner. My guess, however, is that the number of volunteers for any such switch-pulling would be so large that the Israeli government could balance the budget by auctioning off lotto chances to pull it. Personally, I would offer family members of victims of terrorism first "dibs."

Opponents of the death penalty in Israel and elsewhere argue that errors in judgment might be made and innocent people might be executed. This is a fallacious argument even when discussing execution of criminals, but even more so when discussing terrorists. There is no serious evidence I know of that any innocent person has ever been executed in the United States. But more generally, everything we do (and everything government does) carries some risk that an innocent person might be killed as a result of those actions and policies. Should we shut down the post office because postal trucks sometimes run over innocent people? Should we ground all planes because sometimes innocent people are killed in accidents? Even if there were a non-negligible risk of such errors, that is certainly no reason not to have a death penalty.

Opponents of the death penalty argue that it is expensive to implement. This is absurd. Room and board for terrorists for life in prison are exorbitant. The death penalty is "expensive" in the U.S. only because of America's judicial system, which allows endless expensive appeals to proceed forever. Israel has no jury system at all. In any case, these costs can be contained by restricting the options of appeals of convicted terrorists.

"One shouldn't be shocked that the most vociferous opposition to the death penalty for terrorists comes from the same Israeli leftists who always put the rights of Arab murderers ahead of the rights of innocent Jews."

Opponents of the death penalty in Israel argue that terrorists might resist capture by fighting to the death and so harm police and soldiers. I say let's take our chances. Better the soldiers than the children on the school buses or the women in the cafés. That is why we have soldiers. I am sure they will cope. And suicide bombers are not exactly likely to turn more deadly because they face the death penalty if captured.

One shouldn't be shocked that the most vociferous opposition to the death penalty for terrorists comes from the same Israeli leftists who always put the rights of Arab murderers ahead of the rights of innocent Jews. These are the same people who turned most of the West Bank and Gaza Strip into cities of refuge for terrorists, bases for launching murder atrocities against hundreds of Israelis each year.

Periodical Bibliography

The American
Catholic Online
"Capital Punishment and Abortion, an Argument from Doubt," May 3, 2009. http://the-american-catholic.com.

David Benkof
"Fabulously Observant: Jews and the Death Penalty," *Jerusalem Post Online*, March 11, 2009. www.jpost.com.

Mark Beunderman
"Poland Opposes EU Day Against Death Penalty," *EUobserver.com*, May 9, 2007. http://euobserver.com.

Mahua Das
"Capital Punishment: Time to Abandon It?" *Hinduism Today*, October/November/December 2006.

Julio Godoy
"Rights: Death Penalty Better, Say Some, than Slow Execution," *IPS Online*, January 22, 2007. www.ips.org.

Brian Handwerk
"Does Islam Allow for Death Penalty for Converts?" *National Geographic Online*, March 31, 2006. www.nationalgeographic.com.

Soeren Kern
"Europe, America, and the Death Penalty," *GEES Newsletter Online*, January 30, 2007. http://eng.gees.org.

Los Angeles Times
"Mexico Shouldn't Resurrect the Death Penalty," February 5, 2009.

Dan Polish
"Capital Punishment on Trial: Does Judaism Condone Capital Punishment?" *Reform Judaism Magazine*, Summer 2002.

B.A. Robinson
"Death Penalty Policies of Various Religious Groups," *ReligiousTolerance.org*, July 3, 2001. www.religioustolerance.org.

Louise Willis
"Buddhist Nun Speaks Out Against Death Penalty," The World Today Online, August 15, 2003. www.abc.net.au/worldtoday.

GLOBALVIEWPOINTS

CHAPTER 2

Capital Punishment and Public Opinion

In the Caribbean, Citizens Want the Death Penalty Carried Out

Darcus Howe

Darcus Howe is a broadcaster and columnist, who was born in Trinidad and lives in South London. In the following viewpoint, Howe reports on the British Privy Council's trend toward non-capital sentencing for murder cases in the Caribbean. The decisions of the Privy Council are in opposition to the wishes of a large number of people in the Caribbean islands. Howe, however, supports the decisions of the Privy Council.

As you read, consider the following questions:

1. Name three Caribbean countries mentioned in the article.
2. Who makes up the Privy Council?
3. What evidence is given to support the claim that the Caribbean people want the death penalty carried out?

In the English-speaking Caribbean, the death penalty for murder drifts slowly but inexorably into oblivion. Four death-row prisoners, one from Trinidad, two from Barbados and another from Jamaica, applied to the Privy Council, the final court of appeal in Caribbean jurisprudence, to have their

Darcus Howe, "The Caribbean People Like Hanging So Much That They Stone Its Opponents," *New Statesman*, vol. 133, no. 4697, July 19, 2004, p. 18. Copyright © 2004 New Statesman, Ltd. Reproduced by permission.

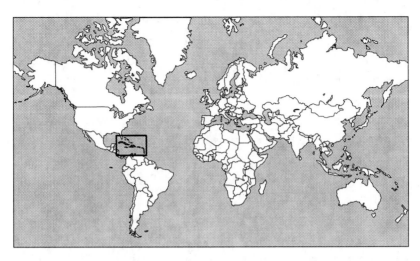

death sentences lifted. Their argument was that there were mitigating factors in their cases, which the islands' judges could not take into account because, once the juries had delivered guilty verdicts, the death penalty was mandatory.

The Privy Council—embodied exceptionally on this occasion in a panel of eight English law lords and one senior judge from Jamaica—ruled that, under the Jamaican constitution, hanging was cruel and degrading. That was not so under the Trinidadian and Barbadian constitutions, the law lords ruled. However, they decided that because, in a previous case, the Privy Council had reached the opposite conclusion for Trinidad and Tobago, those currently on death row in that country should not be hanged.

So 60 prisoners in Jamaica and 100 in Trinidad will escape the rope. It seems to me that in [the] future the Privy Council will find it virtually impossible to uphold a sentence of execution in Trinidad, now that people in similar circumstances have been spared. The shadow of the gallows has not entirely departed from the Caribbean, but it has retreated by some distance. It is admirable that the law lords have put themselves in the vanguard of the movement against capital punishment even though hanging has enormous support among the Caribbean people. A campaigner against hanging in Trinidad was once stoned as he stood picketing alone on a day when several prisoners were executed. The police also turned on him and savagely beat him.

Several Caribbean governments are burning to abolish the Privy Council as the final court of appeal because of its liberal interpretation of the law. It would be replaced by a regional court of appeal, set up for the sole purpose of popping necks, as one former police commissioner in Trinidad described this barbarous act.

Let the Privy Council prevail, I say, along with the fine stock of British lawyers who defend the hapless poor of the Caribbean from barbarism. Despite promises to build anew, many of the old colonial institutions remain intact in the Caribbean. So will the Privy Council, I expect.

In China, Capital Punishment Is Popular for Traditional Reasons

Virgil K. Y. Ho

Virgil K. Y. Ho is a professor of history at the Hong Kong University of Science and Technology. In the following viewpoint, excerpted from the chapter "What Is Wrong with Capital Punishment," Ho argues that Chinese people usually show favor toward the death penalty. Ho argues that the Chinese state does not enforce conformity on this matter. Nonetheless, the Chinese believe strongly that criminals are wicked and deserve death and that the death penalty is applied fairly. These beliefs seem to be linked in part to traditional cultural beliefs about the triumph of good over evil, the morality of divine retribution, and the usefulness of harsh punishment in maintaining social order.

As you read, consider the following questions:

1. Virgil K. Y. Ho had trouble getting people to talk to him about death because he conducted his survey in the weeks before what auspicious event?
2. Who is Judge Bao?
3. What is *zhi luanshi yong zhongdian*?

Virgil K. Y. Ho, "What Is Wrong with Capital Punishment?: Official and Unofficial Attitudes Toward Capital Punishment in Modern and Contemporary China," *The Cultural Lives of Capital Punishment*, Palo Alto, CA: Stanford University Press, 2005, pp. 274–90. Copyright © 2005 by the Board of Trustees of the Leland Stanford Junior University. All rights reserved. Used with the permission of Stanford University Press, www.sup.org.

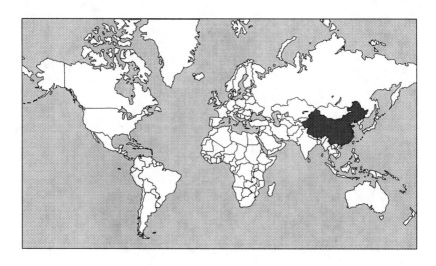

Conducting unofficial interviews with ordinary citizens in the People's Republic of China on the subject of the death penalty was no easy matter, since most of my respondents and informants were initially reluctant to express their views on the subject. This reluctance was the result of three main considerations, which became apparent to me only after I had been acquainted with the informants for some time. First, the issue of the death penalty is generally regarded as something that concerns the State alone and hence is highly sensitive politically. Informants were afraid that any comment they made would contradict the State's position on the issue. Second, most informants were aware that China has been strongly criticized by many human rights groups in the West for her overuse and misuse of the death penalty. Human rights, in their view, was a sensitive issue since the concept of human rights had until recently been renounced by the State as bourgeoise—that is, unmaterialistic and unscientific and, hence, un-Marxist. But what was even more worrying to them was the much-publicized fact that the enemies of China exploit the issue of human rights as a pretext for interfering in the domestic affairs of China.... Therefore, their instinctive reaction to any unofficial or unsolicited inquiry on the subject was to treat it with suspicion. Third, death has never been a popular topic of conversation in China; it was, and to a large extent still is, a culturally taboo subject and therefore is to be avoided if possible.

The respondents' fears and caution, however, were actually groundless and unnecessary. Although the Chinese authorities may not endorse the kind of activity promoted by foreign human rights organizations in China, they do not penalize anyone who holds a different view over the issue of capital punishment, as long as s/he does not transform thoughts into organized collective action or public opinion that challenges the political supremacy of the State. More important, when informants hesitated to express their views on the matter, they were unaware of how similar their opinions actually were to that of their own government.

Among the hesitant informants were a number of mid- and low-ranking government officials and Party cadres. Their initial reticence, as they later explained, was mainly out of a natural instinct for self-protection: it seemed wise to refrain from responding to my inquiries so as to avoid making an ill-judged comment. Their reticence also reflected a failure of communication between the government and its people over the issue. Had the informants been better acquainted with the official position, they might have been more vocal. Their silence signaled more a distrust of the State than a challenge to the official view on the subject. . . .

". . . most of my respondents . . . and informants insisted that China must keep the death penalty because they could not see why it should be abolished."

Popular Dimension

One reason for the initial reluctance of my respondents to discuss capital punishment is that death is still commonly considered a taboo topic, one that should especially be avoided in the weeks before an auspicious event such as Chinese New Year (symbolically associated with regeneration of life) when my survey was conducted. This brings out an interesting aspect of the public's attitudes toward capital punishment— there is a cultural, even supernatural, dimension to their perception of the issue.

The respondents' initial reticence must not be taken as reluctance to make honest or pro-abolition comments on a sensitive issue. On the contrary, most of my respondents (73 out of 86) and informants insisted that China must keep the death penalty because they could not see why it should be abolished. Among these proponents were university students and middle-age professionals, including medical practitioners, university faculty, nurses, and businessmen—the social sector that seems to be most ardently supportive of an abolitionist stance in the West. Given the informal way my opinion survey was conducted, their positive attitude toward capital punishment was by and large spontaneous, and not in the least swayed by any fear of the State as one might have suspected.

There are other reasons for doubting the influence of the State's ideological indoctrination on my respondents' and informants' views on the death penalty. First, Chinese scholarship on the death penalty, no matter how well articulated, is of no concern to these people, who, to my knowledge, have never read, and probably will never read, anything on such an inauspicious subject. They may, however, occasionally have watched reports on television about a "sentencing rally," which seems to have reinforced, rather than shaped, their own original beliefs and attitudes regarding the socio-cultural relevance of capital punishment, since many phrased their supportive comments in largely traditional parlance rather than that of the official media. The influence of tradition is even more apparent when it comes to my observations in the field, where my peasant informants had never thought about the issue. They opined that since capital punishment has been a part of the Chinese penal system since time immemorial, its continuous existence is simply a matter of course. They don't need the State to educate them in recognizing the value of the death penalty.

"Three well-educated respondents even argued strongly for extracting organs from executed convicts for the purpose of transplant; only in this way, they said, could these bad social elements 'make themselves useful to the society.'"

Second, the Chinese State, to my knowledge, has never conducted any mass publicity campaign to "educate" its subjects in the official view of capital punishment. The "public discourse" on the death penalty is largely confined to a small circle of academics, legal experts, and senior officials; the general populace is both uninterested and uninvolved. It is not surprising, therefore, that the people don't always share the view of the State: seven respondents did argue for the abolishment of capital punishment in China, which they considered cruel and inhumane to the convicts and their families. Two of these seven abolitionists also argued that the death penalty is an uncivilized, open violation of the principles of humanitarianism and human freedom.

The overwhelming majority, however, held a highly affirmative view of the punishment. All of them expressed absolute confidence in the death penalty as an efficacious deterrent against crime, and they also regarded it as an effective way of safeguarding the well-being of society and the lives and the properties of law-abiding citizens like themselves, as well as of maintaining the people's confidence in the rule of law. A number of my respondents and informants described convicts on death row as "wicked criminals of the most horrible type," who, as a menace to the society, must be exterminated. One respondent, himself a senior professor at a medical school, compared the crimes committed by criminals punishable by death to cancer cells inside a human body, which would spread and cause fatal damage to its patient if left untreated, so that aggressive surgery was needed to have them eradicated. Capital punishment, according to many, must be employed to shock the populace, in particular the youngsters, who would then learn about the fatal consequence of committing serious crimes. Of the 73 retentionists, only 15 disapproved of public execution, which they favored because they believed it to be the best way to assuage the anger of a victim's family and of those good citizens who are appalled by the wickedness of the criminal. Although some years ago the State announced its intention to replace public execution by shooting with execution by lethal injection in the confines of a prison, this effort to "humanize" or "modernize" capital punishment has not been popularly received—executing these criminals by lethal injection is regarded as unacceptably lenient. Three well-educated respondents even argued strongly for extracting organs from executed convicts for the purpose of transplant; only in this way, they said, could these bad social elements "make themselves useful to the society." My informants in the field, both urban and rural, had never doubted the validity of using an executed convict's organs for medical purposes.

Underlying this approval of capital punishment is a common assumption that those who are sentenced to death must be the most wicked criminals whose crimes are of the most sinister type. In other words, these convicts deserve no pity and their death is an occasion for joy. People in China also have faith in the fairness and impartiality of the law and the judicial system, though their confidence is not unqualified. Over half the respondents supporting the death penalty admitted that they had worried about miscarriages of justice because of the common problem of corruption in Chinese officialdom. A few respondents learned about such injustice from an interesting source: a highly popular television drama series

Nations Which Executed the Most People in 2007	
Country	Number of People Executed
China	470+
Iran	317+
Saudi Arabia	143+
Pakistan	135+
United States	42+

TAKEN FROM: Amnesty International USA, "Death Penalty Statistics," 2008. www. amnestyusa.org.

about the good deeds of the legendary Judge Bao (999–1062 A.D.), who is a household name for his incorruptible character and unswerving determination to redress countless cases of miscarriage of justice. But in spite of their doubts about the integrity of the legal system, their faith in the efficacy and the ethical justifications of capital punishment remained unshaken. There was no shortage of people who had total trust in the State's legal and penal systems. Two respondents argued that the occasional occurrence of a false accusation must not be taken as evidence of a failure of the system as a whole. The death penalty, they argued, given all its advantages, must be enforced regardless of such "minor" shortcomings—nothing is perfect, and sacrifice must be made at times.

The reference to Judge Bao is interesting because it shows how people still think about the issue of capital punishment in terms of traditional cultural idioms, despite decades of rule by a totalitarian iconoclastic regime. The resurrection of the cult of Judge Bao since the 1990s, which was initiated unexpectedly by a Taiwanese TV melodrama series, not only reminded my respondents and informants of the potential danger of a false charge, but also reinforced their faith in the validity of a traditional religio-cultural tenet: the ultimate triumph of good over evil. This conviction was important because it helped people construe the drama and the reality of capital punishment in ways determined by the story. In the historical dramas about Judge Bao, all the falsely accused eventually clear their names and are acquitted. Miscarriage of justice, as "proven" in drama and perhaps even in real life, is at best only a remote possibility in the eyes of the viewers. Part of the reason for the huge success of the TV show in South China may be that it helps people cope with their worries about the possibility of sending an innocent man to death. It is interesting that the five respondents who opined against the death penalty gave human rights and compassion rather than a possible miscarriage of justice as the reasons for their concern. Moreover, many respondents and informants questioned the validity of concerns about miscarriage of justice, dismissing them as ungrounded and an overreaction. In their view, the legal and penal systems in China are sophisticated enough to have safeguards against false charges or miscarriage of justice. Most important, they don't believe that a truly innocent person can be easily framed, falsely charged, and sentenced to death without arousing the notice of the State and the legal authorities. . . .

"The legal and penal systems in China are sophisticated enough to have safeguards against false charges or miscarriage of justice."

In the discourse of such retentionists, since China has a long history of capital punishment and an old popular belief in divine retributive justice, there is neither sound reason nor imminent need to uproot this aspect of Chinese cultural tradition. A foreign correspondent reported "that even the most sophisticated urbanites would shrink from the idea of abolishing capital punishment altogether. 'There is a Chinese saying that you should kill the chicken to scare the monkeys,' says [a] university graduate. . . . 'We need that threat to be there—it's part of our culture.'". . .

Capital punishment is popularly perceived and justified in the name of history, tradition, and Chinese culture. The combined effect of these popular perceptions of the death penalty apparently reinforces the impression that all those who are sentenced to death by the court must be criminals of the most wicked or sinister kind who deserve to be exterminated. The fact that those who sentenced to death include people who have committed more minor, nonviolent crimes, such as corruption, trafficking in women, robbery, negligence resulting in a fatal industrial accident, and so on, doesn't seem to have bothered retentionists. Most respondents and informants maintained that since these criminals are wicked or evil, they must not be treated like ordinary people and in accordance with the principle of humanitarianism. These criminals, they opined, are themselves the violators of the principle of humanitarianism in their criminal acts. Accordingly, if these wicked criminals and murderers are not punished by death in public, the relatives of the victims of their crimes are not treated humanitarianly either. To some informants, even putting a "wicked criminal" of this type on trial was a waste of public resources and time; these "subhumans" should be "shot on the spot."

The traditional attitude of "an eye to an eye" and retribution is commonly considered to be apt and fair and not at odds with the ideal or principle of humanitarianism. Although many informants were aware of criticisms of China's practice of capital punishment by Western human rights groups, most of those I spoke with did not support abolition in China. They argued that since crime in China shows no sign of abating in the current volatile socio-economic and political environments, the old Chinese wisdom that "severe penal codes are the answer to social disorder" (*zhi luanshi yong zhongdian*, a tenet of Chinese statecraft with a long history dating back at least to the time of Confucius, 511–479 B.C.) is still proper for China. They believed that since this tenet had helped China maintain a peaceful and orderly society in the past, its continuous relevance to the present-date China was undeniable. They also believed that since most people were for the death penalty, any abolitionist talk was a clear deviation from social responsibility, or what is commonly considered to be the right thing to do for maintaining a better society. . . .

This chapter set out to look for similarities and differences between the official and the popular attitudes toward capital punishment in modern China. My finding is that there are large areas of similarity, along with occasional areas of difference, in officials' and civilians' views of the death penalty. An insignificantly small number of officials and legal experts questioned the socio-political appropriateness of the death penalty. The majority of my informants and respondents supported capital punishment unreservedly, regarding it as essential for their country. The prevalence of this attitude is not necessarily to be attributed just to the ideological indoctrination imposed by the State upon its people; the regime hasn't launched any intensive publicity campaign in this respect, and the people need no such propaganda to shape their views of the socio-cultural and political meanings of the death penalty. My informants' opinions indicated that their feelings about capital punishment stemmed, not from the State's propaganda or from schools, but mainly from old cultural values embedded and disseminated through old history books or vernacular novels and theatrical and oral traditions. Somewhat ironically, history and tradition are thus utilized as twin towers to legitimize and justify China's continuous application of the death penalty in the modern age. Most of my respondents and informants did not see a contradiction between the practice of capital punishment and the ideals of humanitarianism, human rights, nonviolence, and modernization (or globalization).

On the contrary, there seems to be a strong public consensus in China about the efficacy and desirability of capital punishment as a means of safeguarding these "modern," noble ideals, which are reserved only for law-abiding citizens. Such popular acceptance explains why the State's position on capital punishment is never seriously questioned; in the long history of capital punishment in China since antiquity, neither the elite nor the commoners have questioned its social, cultural, and political importance. The Chinese State has in the course of its history been concerned to abolish specific forms of cruel capital punishment, but the fundamental idea of the death penalty has never been challenged. . . .

In the view of the majority, there is nothing ethically or socio-culturally wrong with the legal principle of capital punishment. For most Chinese in China (including Taiwan), the death penalty has served, and still serves, a meaningful purpose for their country and its people.

In Indonesia, the Popularity of the Death Penalty Makes Abolition Unlikely

Community of Sant'Egidio

The Community of Sant'Egidio is a an officially recognized Catholic lay community. It is involved in many humanitarian projects, including anti-death penalty advocacy. In the following viewpoint, the community notes that executions and the number of people on death row in Indonesia have increased rapidly in recent years. Both the government and the people strongly support the death penalty, whether for murder or drug offenses. The Constitutional Court has ruled against abolitionists in several key cases. Given popular support and legal defeats, Indonesia seems likely to continue to execute prisoners for the foreseeable future.

As you read, consider the following questions:

1. By what method are condemned prisoners executed in Indonesia?

2. According to a Media Indonesia poll in 2006, which category of crime did Indonesians believe most deserved the death penalty?

3. What key change in the death penalty do drafters say is being included in the revision of the Indonesian Criminal Code?

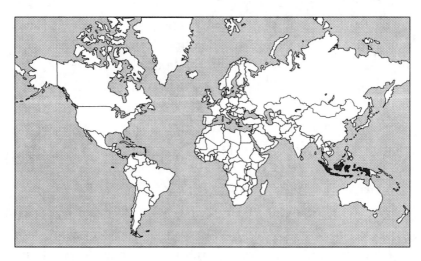

The year 2008 has been a dismal one for opponents of the death penalty in Indonesia. Ten people have been executed, almost equaling the number of executions in Indonesia during the preceding decade. The Constitutional Court also rejected a challenge to the 1964 law governing the method of execution, after last year [2007] also rejecting a challenge to the constitutionality of the death penalty for narcotics crimes. With an election next year, around 100 people still on death row and few avenues left to challenge the legality of capital punishment, there could still be more executions to come.

Executions in Indonesia Set to Increase

Indonesia is one of 60 countries that retains the death penalty, according to Amnesty International figures (137 have abolished capital punishment in law or in practice). As Indonesia ratified the International Covenant on Civil and Political Rights in 2005, it may only impose the death penalty for 'the most serious crimes'. In Indonesia's interpretation, terrorism, premeditated murder and grave human rights violations all fall within 'the most serious crimes'. Somewhat unusually, narcotics offences and corruption do as well.

Executions in Indonesia are carried out by firing squad, and typically take place late at night in secret locations. Condemned prisoners are informed 72 hours before their execution is to take place. A police firing squad shoots the prisoner in the heart from a distance of between five and 10 metres, upon the signal of a swift downward sword stroke from the squad commander. If the prisoner is still alive, the deputy squad commander then presses the muzzle of his gun on the prisoner's head and fires a 'finishing shot'.

With almost twice as many people on death row as have been executed in the past 30 years, Indonesia will soon have to conduct a lot more executions, or it will have to commute many or all of the sentences.

"The death penalty appears to enjoy widespread support in Indonesia, both in government ranks and among the general public."

On the one hand, judicial executions in Indonesia may appear to be a relatively minor problem. Indonesia is generally estimated to have executed just over 50 people since the late 1970s; in the same period the United States has carried out more than 1000 executions. Even within Indonesia, a far greater number of people have perished in extrajudicial killings during the same time frame. For instance, death squads summarily executed several thousand suspected criminals and urban thugs during the Suharto [president from 1967–1998] regime's infamous Petrus—or mysterious killings—campaign in the early 1980s.

But Indonesia has reached a crossroads as far as capital punishment is concerned. With almost twice as many people on death row as have been executed in the past 30 years, either it will soon have to conduct a lot more executions, or it will have to commute many or all of these sentences.

Indonesians Support the Death Penalty

The death penalty appears to enjoy widespread support in Indonesia, both in government ranks and among the general public. No systematic data on public opinion is available, but media polls typically show around 75 percent support for capital punishment. The results of some of these polls may surprise foreign readers. For instance, a 2006 poll in the national Media Indonesia daily found 78 percent support for the death penalty for terrorists, 78 percent for drug dealers, 68 percent for people involved in large-scale corruption and 67 percent for murderers. When asked to rank which out of these four categories of crime most deserved the death penalty, drug offences ranked narrowly behind corruption and terrorism, with murder a distant last.

The Indonesian government has also repeatedly stated its firm support for retention of the death penalty. In its submission to the Constitutional Court case on capital punishment for narcotics crime, for example, the Ministry of Law and Human Rights argued that the death penalty was an essential part of the government's law enforcement arsenal. The death penalty was used only in specific circumstances, for the most heinous crimes, and was applied selectively, only when guilt had been proved beyond reasonable doubt, the ministry said. Quoting the Attorney General, the government also submitted that the weak state of Indonesia's law enforcement bodies meant that abolishing the death penalty would worsen the law and order situation in Indonesia, and send the wrong message to drug dealers.

Ironically, opponents of the death penalty cite the same facts in arguing for abolition. To retain the death penalty when Indonesia's legal system is so weak, the applicants in the Constitutional Court case submitted, runs the risk that innocent people will be wrongly convicted and executed.

The Abolition Campaign in Indonesia Has Not Been Successful

Some executions in Indonesia have attracted widespread protest. The execution of three Catholic men in 2006 in connection with the Poso conflict [religious violence between Christians and Muslims in the town of Poso] and the recent executions of three of the Bali bombers [convicted of attacks on resort nightclubs in 2002] were each preceded by demonstrations and media controversy. For each of these executions, though, most opposition derived from the specific background of the case rather than being motivated by rejection of the death penalty per se. Many of those who protested over these cases would be unlikely to campaign for abolition of the death penalty in all cases.

A small but committed abolitionist movement is working to end capital punishment in Indonesia, however. The movement centres on human rights NGOs [nongovernmental organizations], religious figures and certain academics. 'We had hoped that after the reform movement in 1998 [when Suharto was forced out of office by mass demonstrations] it would be easy to get rid of the death penalty,' said Rusdi Marpaung, managing director of Imparsial and a member of the Coalition for the Abolition of the Death Penalty, when I spoke to him recently. 'But it didn't turn out to be the case. The Criminal Code left by the Dutch [the major colonial power in Indonesia] remained in place.' . . .

Abolition Has Suffered Defeats in Court

But two setbacks in the Constitutional Court have left the abolitionist movement with few options. Last year [2007], the Constitutional Court rejected a challenge to the death penalty in narcotics cases that was brought by three Australians sentenced to death for drug offences and two Indonesian applicants. The Court reasoned that the non-derogable right to life guaranteed in Article 28I(1) of the Indonesian constitution

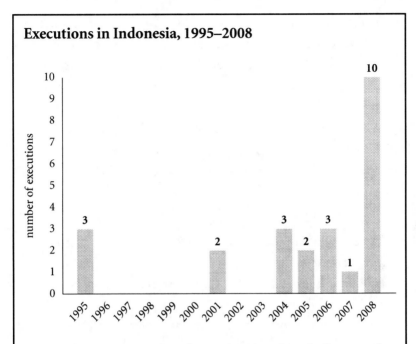

Executions in Indonesia, 1995–2008

TAKEN FROM: Tim Goodwin, "Executions in Indonesia Since 1995," *Asia Death Penalty*, September 26, 2006. www.asiadeathpenalty.blogspot.com; Amnesty International USA, "Indonesia: Make Today's Executions the Last," November 8, 2008. www.amnestyusa.org.

was subject to the restrictions on human rights in Article 28J(2). The latter article states that an individual's rights are subject to restriction to protect the rights of others. The Court also stated that particular narcotics crimes could rightly be considered to be 'the most serious crimes'. There was no substantive difference between particularly serious narcotics crimes on the one hand, and genocide or crimes against humanity on the other, the court said, as each posed 'a danger of incalculable gravity' and could undermine the 'economic, cultural and political foundations of society'.

Admittedly, the Court's decision in this case was not unanimous. Three of the nine justices filed dissenting opinions on the constitutionality of the death penalty. But only one of these judges is still on the court today.

In a second case this year [2008], the Court unanimously upheld the constitutionality of execution by firing squad. Lawyers acting for the Bali bombers had charged that death by firing squad did not guarantee instant death, and so amounted to torture. In rejecting the challenge, the Court agreed with the government's argument that the pain caused by execution could not be considered to be torture, because generating this pain was merely an inevitable by-product of the lawful act of executing a prisoner.

"There was no substantive difference between particularly serious narcotics crimes on the one hand, and genocide or crimes against humanity on the other, the court said. . . ."

Activists could also lobby for the death penalty to be abolished as part of ongoing revisions to the Criminal Code. Here, also, the prospects are poor. Two members of the drafting team for the new law testified in the Constitutional Court that they had decided to retain the death penalty for the same offences to which it currently applies. One key change that the drafters did say will be included in the new code is that judges will be able to set a 10-year probation period as part of a death sentence, after which the sentence would either be commuted or carried out based on the behaviour of the prisoner in the intervening period. Any such change must still be debated by the parliament, however. The substance of the draft law apart, the revision process has already dragged on for years, and it is far from clear when a new criminal code will finally be enacted. . . .

Meanwhile Indonesian courts continue to hand down death sentences at a swift rate, with at least 14 people added to death row this year [2008].

There Will Be More Executions

Ten executions so far this year [2008] and an election next year [2009] both point to more executions in the short term. The government may even start to take more serious moves to execute everyone on death row. The Constitutional Court called for as much in handing down its judgment on the Narcotics Law, recommending imminent executions of all death row prisoners who had exhausted their avenues of appeal. But nothing in Indonesian law dictates a timetable for a death sentence to be carried out, and the wait for a death row prisoner could be anything from months to years. High profile cases may proceed to execution more quickly, but often it is not clear why a particular case reaches the front of the queue [line].

"The government may even start to take more serious moves to execute everyone on death row."

Comparison of three executions carried out in July this year [2008] illustrates the variation in timing. Yusuf Maulana, a sorcerer (dukun) [or traditional witch doctor] convicted of murdering eight of his patients, was sentenced to death in March 2008. By contrast, Sumiarsih and Sugeng, executed just two hours after Yusuf, were convicted of murder in 1988. And in 2007, the national daily *Kompas* turned up the case of Matar—convicted of multiple murder, rape and robbery—still on death row after his first plea for clemency was rejected in 1972.

The death penalty in Indonesia appears to be here to stay. But the future for those on death row is less certain.

Governments with Popular Support Are More Likely to Abolish the Death Penalty

Carsten Anckar

Carsten Anckar is a professor of political science at Mid-Sweden University and Åbo Akademi University in Finland. In the following viewpoint, he states that public opinion in Europe supports the death penalty, though elites have abolished it. Anckar suggests that democratic governments have broad support, and therefore are sometimes willing to go against popular opinion on moral issues. Authoritarian governments, however, are more insecure and reluctant to abolish the popular death penalty. Since Islam specifically supports the death penalty, authoritarian Islamic countries are especially unlikely to abolish capital punishment.

As you read, consider the following questions:

1. According to Carsten Anckar, what percentage of the population of Sweden supports the death penalty?

2. According to Anckar, what is the ultimate reason for many non-democratic governments holding on to the death penalty?

3. In purely Islamic societies, according to Anckar, what regulates all aspects of life?

Carsten Anckar, *Determinants of the Death Penalty: A Comparative Study of the World.* Andover, Hampshire: Routledge, 2004, pp. 168–71. Copyright © 2004 Carsten Anckar. Reproduced by permission of the publisher.

At least from a European perspective, it is evident that international pressure to abolish the death penalty grows stronger all the time. The attitude toward capital punishment has sharpened, especially during the last two decades. The United Nations and the European Union in particular are forerunners in the abolitionist movement. Among (Western) European politicians, there is wide agreement on the negative attitude toward the death penalty. This, however, is the European view. When we travel across the Atlantic, quite another picture emerges. The attitude toward the death penalty is generally more favorable among politicians and it is probably fair to say that, for a serious contender for the US presidency, it would be political suicide to take a stand against the death penalty.

European People Support the Death Penalty

Apparently, then, there is a strong discrepancy between the attitude toward the death penalty in Europe and in the United States. However, a more careful consideration suggests that this is not necessarily the case. Attitudes toward the death penalty are regularly measured in opinion polls both in Europe and in America. Although Americans tend to have a more favorable attitude toward capital punishment than Europeans, it is clear that the wide consensus of complete deprecation of capital punishment by the governments of European countries is not always mirrored in the population at large. For instance, in a number of European countries, opinions polls show that a majority was in favor of the death penalty at the time of abolition and that support for the death penalty continues to be high.

It is telling that even in a country like Sweden, where capital punishment has not been a political issue for decades and where virtually every politician from right to left condemns the use of the death penalty, figures suggest that not less than

33 percent of the population is in favor of the death penalty. The figure of 33 percent becomes even more interesting when we compare it with the proportion of the population in favor of the beating of children as a method of discipline within the home, which is 9 percent. It is indeed remarkable that a substantial proportion of the population believes that the government should have the right to kill its citizens, but a much smaller proportion is ready to allow parents to smack their children. It is also evident that popular demands for the death penalty are sensitive to general modes of security and that general opinion varies, particularly in times when society is affected by heinous crimes.

"In a strictly Islamic country, the hands of the governments are tied. . . . The death penalty is not only an option, it is an obligation."

Legitimate Governments Can More Easily Oppose Public Opinion

It is thus evident that, as far as the attitude toward the death penalty is concerned, there is a gap between the elite and the masses. However, it must be emphasized that this gap is probably deeper in democracies than in authoritarian societies. Although reliable results of opinion polls are difficult to come across for authoritarian countries, it is fair to assume that both rulers and the ruled share a positive view of the death penalty (at least as long as the punishment is not applied for political crimes). Consequently, a very interesting picture emerges. In one form of government, popular opinion should play a crucial role for the governing body, namely in democracies. Nevertheless, with regard to one policy area, the death penalty, this is not the case. With regard to this issue, the elite have turned a deaf ear to public demands. Why, then, do governments in democracies feel there is no need to respond to popular demands for the death penalty?

One plausible explanation, which is not very far-fetched, has to do with the different bases of legitimacy that democratic and authoritarian governments stand on. In a democracy, the ruling class knows it has come to power by means of popular elections. When the majority of the population constitutes your basis of support, you can allow yourself to go against popular demands as long as you are convinced you have a moral obligation to do so. After the fall of the Soviet Union, the legitimacy of non-democratic forms of government has been questioned. Nowadays, international pressure on authoritarian governments can sometimes be very hard indeed. In situations where authoritarian governments face the difficult task of legitimating their rule, it is difficult to see why they should confront the population in an issue which does not constitute a threat to its rule. Evidently, this line of reasoning probably performs better in explaining why democratic governments remain unperturbed by popular demands for capital punishment than why authoritarian governments uphold the death penalty. For many non-democratic governments, the ultimate reason for holding on to the death penalty is probably that this form of punishment is an effective tool for keeping a firm grip on the society.

Islam Legitimizes the Death Penalty

The issue of legitimacy becomes very important indeed, however, for one category of non-democratic countries—the Islamic countries. In Islamic countries the legitimacy of the death penalty rests on a solid base. In purely Islamic societies, all aspects of life are regulated by the Sharia [Islamic law]. Thus, there is no separation of the religious from the political sphere. . . . The Koran is unequivocal with regard to the death penalty and capital punishment is prescribed for a number of crimes. In a strictly Islamic country, the hands of the governments are tied when the issue of capital punishment is raised. The death penalty is not only an option, it is an obligation.

Support by Country for the Execution of Saddam Hussein, Iraqi Dictator Sentenced to Death in December 2006

Country	Support for Death Sentence
United States	82%
Britain	69%
France	58%
Germany	53%
Spain	51%
Italy	46%

TAKEN FROM: Angus Reid Global Monitor, "Most Americans Support Hussein's Execution," December 26, 2006. www.angus_reid.com.

One could, of course, object to this line of reasoning and claim that the Old Testament also prescribes the death penalty for a number of crimes. The crucial difference between governments in Islamic countries and in Christian countries, however, is that the latter do not have to confront the Sharia.

This means that if decision makers in Islamic countries were to abolish the death penalty, they would have to confront not only the majority of the population, but also the fundamental values on which the whole Islamic society is built. Needless to say, this is an insurmountable task to any power-holder. The legitimacy of the death penalty is deeply rooted in Islamic tradition, and it is not venturesome to predict that, in this category of countries, the abolitionist movement has a very difficult task indeed. The combination of authoritarian rule and the positive attitude toward the death penalty in the Koran is of particular interest. On the one hand, power-holders are likely to regard the death penalty as a useful tool for keeping ... [their] grip on society. As long as tradition and religion supports this view, public opinion will not work against capital punishment. Thus, to put it bluntly, the future of the death penalty looks bright in Islamic countries.

Positive Death Penalty Attitudes May Affect Decisions on Non-Capital Sentencing

Stuart J. McKelvie

Stuart J. McKelvie is a professor in the Psychology Department at Bishop's University in Quebec, Canada. In this viewpoint, McKelvie reports on a study that tests whether a positive attitude toward capital punishment affects other sentencing decisions. If such a realtionship could be established, it could shed light on the view that a positive attitude toward capital punishment reflects conservatism and authoritarianism traits and values, with the expectation that those with such traits and values would be more likely to recommend the death penalty when it is an option as well as a more severe method of execution or a longer prison term and harsher terms of parole in non-death-penalty situations, and to evaluate the actions of the accused as intended. The study found that people with positive attitudes toward captial punishment were in fact more likely (than those with negative opinions of the death penalty) to vote for the death penalty when it was an option, to impose harsher penalties in non-capital sentencing cases, and to take the circumstances of the crime into consideration.

Stuart J. McKelvie, "Attitude Toward Capital Punishment Is Related to Capital and Non-Capital Sentencing," *North American Journal of Psychology*, vol. 8, no. 3, December 2006, pp. 567–590. Copyright © 2006 *North American Journal of Psychology*. Reproduced by permission.

As you read, consider the following questions:

1. How many people participated as subjects in McKelvie's experiment?
2. What role did gender play in the sentencing results?
3. What result of the study turned out contrary to expectation, in that a positive attitude toward capital punishment did not lead to significantly harsher sentencing?

Two hundred and twenty eight Canadian undergraduates read one of two crime vignettes that varied in how justified a murder seemed to be, then made capital (death penalty), capital-related (method of execution), and non capital (prison term, granting of parole, waiting period before parole) sentencing recommendations. Compared to people with a negative attitude toward capital punishment, people with a positive attitude were more severe for both the capital and non capital judgments. They were also harsher for the less than for the more justifiable crime, whereas people with a negative attitude gave similar judgments in each case. Women were generally harsher than men. It is suggested that members of juries chosen to be death-qualified may be biased in any non capital recommendations and that attitude toward capital punishment may reflect other personality traits and values that determine how generally harsh a person's recommended punishment will be.

When a defendant is found guilty, the judgment and subsequent sentence should be based on evidential factors such as crime seriousness and the degree of criminal responsibility (Mazzella & Feingold, 1994). That is, using legally-admissable evidence, punishment should be harsher for crimes that are more serious than those that are less serious, and for people who planned the crime and carried it out intentionally than for those who acted less deliberately. Severity of punishment might also depend on the circumstances in which the crime was committed, particularly if the defendant is judged to have had some justification for committing the crime. Other extra-legal factors may also influence offender treatment. Some of these, such as the employment status or sex of the defendant, may be appropriate on utilitarian grounds because they are thought to predict recidivism (Gebotys & Roberts, 1987). For example, an employed person has a lower risk of re-offending than an unemployed person and so may be given a lighter sentence than an unemployed person. However, other factors, such as defendant attractiveness (Mazzella & Feingold, 1994), represent bias and are unacceptable. For example, people who are more attractive have been judged more leniently than people who are less attractive (Mazzella & Feingold, 1994).

These factors refer to the offender, but some refer to the judge and jury, who are often permitted considerable discretion when deciding punishment (Wheeler, Weisburd & Bode, 1982). One of these personal characteristics is attitude toward capital punishment, which may be an acceptable or an unacceptable extralegal factor, depending on the nature of the sentence. For example, as long as a death penalty recommendation follows the law, courts in the United States accept that jurors' attitude towards capital punishment will be related to their verdict, because the death penalty could never be rendered by people who are not "death qualified" (O'Neil, Patry, & Penrod, 2004). However, it would not be appropriate for attitude towards capital punishment to influence non capital sentences.

Furthermore, it would not be appropriate for any sentencing decision to be related to subject factors such as the sex, personality traits or political values of people making judgments. Unfortunately, there is evidence of this kind of bias. For sex, men are usually harsher than women when recommending the death penalty in a specific case (Honeyman & Ogloff, 1996). Although studies show no relationship between sex and length of prison sentence (McKelvie, Mitchell, Arnot, & Sullivan, 1993; Riedel, 1993), some show that men are harsher (McKelvie, 2002) and others show that women are harsher (McNamara, Vattano, & Viney, 1993).

With regard to personality and values, people who are high in authoritarianism have recommended more severe punishment than those who are low (Gerbasi, Zuckerman, & Reis, 1977), particularly if they perceive themselves to have different attitudes than the defendant (Mitchell & Byrne, 1973). Authoritarianism in the person judging and their attitude similarity with the offender have also been related to their attributions of responsibility and leniency of treatment (Feather, 2002). Furthermore, conservatives have been found to be more punitive than liberals and to be more likely to attribute the defendant's actions to internal than to external causes (Davis, Severy, Kraus, & Whitaker, 1993; Vidmar, 1974). In the latter case, intention, which is normally an evidential factor, becomes an extralegal factor, because the attribution is biased by personal characteristics of the judge.

Furthermore, it would not be appropriate for any sentencing decision to be related to subject factors such as the sex, personality traits or political values of people making judgments. Unfortunately, there is evidence of this kind of bias.

The main purpose of the present study was to investigate the relationship between attitude toward capital punishment and sentencing severity, which has both practical and theoretical implications. Although it would be expected and acceptable that attitude towards capital punishment would be related to a death penalty recommendation, attitude towards capital punishment should not be related to non capital sentencing. As noted above, jurors in the United States are usually screened in capital cases, and this may also occur in other countries (Mauro, 1992). That is, jurors are not permitted to serve unless they are "death-qualified," which essentially means that they must be willing to vote for a death sentence when that is an option (Horowitz & Seguin, 1986; Mauro, 1992). Of course, this does not mean that they will recommend it, only that they would not exclude it from consideration. The practical implication of the present research is that if attitude towards capital punishment is related in general to sentencing severity, it introduces a source of bias towards more severe non capital recommendations when the jury is selected to be death-qualified (Mauro, 1992). Indeed, it has been found that death-qualified jurors are more likely to convict than people who would be excluded from capital cases (Horowitz & Seguin, 1986; Mauro 1992; although for a dissenting view, see Elliot, 1992).

It was noted above that sentencing decisions have been related to personality traits and political values. The present results are of theoretical interest because it has been suggested that belief in the death penalty reflects these traits and values (Stack, 2000). For example, Eysenck (1954) argued that belief in capital punishment was based on the trait of radicalism/ conservatism. In addition, compared to people who oppose the death penalty, those who believe in it are more authoritarian (Ray, 1982; Stack, 2000; Vidmar, 1974), less liberal (Stack, 2000), and less tolerant (Valliant & Oliver, 1997). Like conservatives compared to liberals, they are also more likely than opponents of capital punishment to judge that the act was intended (Goodman-Delahunty, Greene, & Hsiao, 1998).

If attitude toward capital punishment reflects such traits and values, it might be expected that people in favour of capital punishment would be generally harsher in their sentencing judgments than those who are against it. That is, because they favour capital punishment, they would be more likely to recommend the death penalty, and possibly a more severe method of execution, but they might also recommend longer prison terms and be more severe in granting parole. In fact, consistent with this argument, and like death-qualified jurors, people who believe in capital punishment are more likely to convict than those who are against it (Allen, Mabry, & McKelton, 1998). In addition, belief in capital punishment might not only be related to perceived intention, but also to other attributions. For example, people who are in favor of capital punishment may judge that the offender was less justified in their action and less driven to it. Such findings have additional theoretical implications, because it has been proposed that attitude towards capital punishment may have an indirect effect on capital sentencing via its relationship with attributions (O'Neil et al., 2004). That is, people with a stronger belief in capital punishment may evaluate the motives of the accused more harshly than people with a weaker belief, leading them to be more likely to recommend the death penalty.

On the other hand, past research has shown that attitudes are a better predictor of behaviour if the two domains share the same level of specificity (Newcomb, Rabow, & Hernandez, 1992). Belief in the death penalty may be a fairly specific attitude, so that those who are pro would be more likely to recommend capital punishment than those are con, but they might not be more severe in other recommendations pertaining to jail time and parole (and perhaps method of execution), and they might not differ in their attributions.

Participants then read one of two cases in which the accused had already been found guilty of a planned murder. In both conditions, the defendant killed a man whom he felt was responsible for his brother's death, but they differed according to the circumstances under which the act occurred.

This review shows that people with a more positive attitude toward capital punishment and people who are death qualified are more likely to convict an offender and to perceive that their action was intended than people with a more negative attitude and people who are excludable. The present experiment extends this work by examining the relationship between attitude toward capital punishment and three kinds of sentencing recommendation: capital (death penalty), capital-related (execution method), and non capital (prison term, granting of parole, waiting period before parole). The relationship between attitude toward capital punishment and three kinds of attribution (justification, being driven to act, intent) was also investigated.

Participants began by completing a questionnaire that measured their attitude toward capital punishment. Although there has been some disagreement over whether attitudes should be defined as composed of three components (cognition, affect, behavioral tendency) or only one (affect) (Brigham, 1991, p. 134), the present instrument consisted of statements about belief in capital punishment. As such, it emphasized the cognitive component of the attitude. Participants then read one of two cases in which the accused had already been found guilty of a planned murder. In both conditions, the defendant killed a man whom he felt was responsible for his brother's death, but they differed according to the circumstances under which the act occurred. In one case (killing circumstances), which was expected to be perceived as more justified, the murder victim was a hit man who had himself been accused of killing the brother. In the other (job circumstances), the defendant's brother died suddenly after discovering that his application for a job had been unsuccessful. The murder victim was the person who obtained the position over the defendant's brother. After reading the crime scenarios, participants gave sentencing recommendations then their attributions.

Because the defendant had been found guilty of the murder, it was expected that attitude toward capital punishment would be directly related to the likelihood that the death penalty was recommended. However, the relationship might be stronger in the job circumstances than in the killing circumstances. In the first case, where the offender would be perceived as having very little or no justification for his action, people who had a negative attitude to capital punishment would not recommend it, but people who had a positive attitude would be quite likely to do so. In the second case, where the offender would be perceived as more justified in his action, people with a negative attitude would again not recommend it, but people with a positive might be only slightly more likely to do so.

However, the major question here was whether attitude toward capital punishment would also be related to the capital-related and to the non capital recommendations for punishment and to attributions concerning the criminal act. If people with a positive attitude toward capital punishment are generally harsher than those with a negative attitude, the capital-related and non capital recommendations would follow the same pattern as the capital recommendations. In addition, although the scenarios described both murders as deliberate, which implies that perceived intention would be very high and similar for all participants, people with a positive attitude towards capital punishment might be more likely to perceive the act as intended than people with a negative attitude. Finally, people with a positive attitude might be less likely to perceive the offender as justified or driven to commit the act than those with a negative attitude.

A secondary interest in the present study was sex of participant. In view of the research cited above, it was expected that men would have a more positive attitude toward capital punishment than women and would be more likely to render a death sentence. However, no prediction was made concerning sex differences in the capital-related or non capital judgments, or in the attributions. . . .

Discussion

As predicted, people with a positive attitude towards capital punishment were more likely to recommend the death penalty than those with a negative attitude, and this effect was stronger in the job circumstances where the victim was fairly appointed to a professional position than in the killing circumstances where the victim was a former hit man who himself had been tried for murder.... The reason for expecting that the effect would be stronger in the first case was that the murder of a man who was appointed fairly to a job would be seen as less justified and therefore more punishable than the murder of a man who had himself been accused of a killing. Indeed, participants rated the murder in the job circumstances as less justified than in the killing circumstances, and they also rated that offender as less driven to his action in the job circumstances. Furthermore, participants' capital and non capital recommendations were both harsher in the job circumstances than in the killing circumstances. These results demonstrate that people with a positive attitude toward capital punishment were more likely to recommend the death penalty for a specific crime than people with a negative attitude, and that they took the circumstances into account. In fact, as predicted, people with a negative attitude were unlikely to recommend the death penalty in either scenario, whereas those with a positive attitude were more likely to recommend it than those with a negative attitude in the killing circumstances, and were also more likely to recommend it in the job circumstances than in the killing circumstances. Although attitude toward capital punishment is an extralegal factor, its relationship to the death penalty recommendation is acceptable, because in countries which retain capital punishment, juries are usually death-qualified. (O'Neil et al., 2004). However, any relationship to other kinds of recommendations are not acceptable, and represent a bias in judgment.

The main purpose of the present study was to examine this question by establishing whether attitude toward capital punishment was associated with harshness of punishment in general. For the method of execution, which was not itself a capital judgment but was related to it, people with a positive attitude toward capital punishment chose a slightly more severe method than those with a negative attitude. . . . However, this difference was only marginally significant by the conventional standard. . . . Overall, the strong relationship between attitude toward capital punishment and death penalty recommendation did not generalize to the method of execution. One reason for this may be that most people chose lethal injection for humanitarian reasons. . . .

It was found that people with a positive attitude toward capital punishment did perceive the murder as more intended than people with a negative attitude. . . . However, there was no relationship between attitude toward capital punishment and the offender being driven.

However, for the non capital recommendations, which included prison time, granting of parole, and waiting time before parole, the results were similar to those for the capital recommendation. . . . Most important, it was found that the effects of attitude towards capital punishment and the interaction between crime circumstances and attitude toward capital punishment were significant. . . . People with a positive attitude toward capital punishment were harsher than people with a negative attitude, and this effect was stronger in the job circumstances than in the killing circumstances. . . . These results show that the relationship between attitude toward capital punishment and capital recommendations generalized to non capital recommendations. They suggest that people with a positive attitude toward capital punishment would be likely to render harsher prison terms and parole recommendations than those with a negative attitude. Because this would not be acceptable under the law, it demonstrates an extralegal factor that is a source of bias in judgment (Mauro, 1992). Practically, the results imply that if a death-qualified jury did not make a capital recommendation, it would be likely to recommend harsher non capital punishment than a jury that was not death-qualified.

These findings are also consistent with previous research demonstrating that people who believe in capital punishment and jurors who are death-qualified are more likely to convict an accused person than people who are opposed and not death qualified (Allen, et al., 1998; Horowitz & Seguin, 1986; Mauro 1992). However, they extend past research to the second stage of jury deliberations where sentencing occurs. In most capital court cases, the same jurors reach a verdict then, at a later time, make a sentencing recommendation (a bifurcated system, Horowitz & Seguin, 1986). The results are relevant to the suggestion that different juries be employed in the two phases (Horowitz & Seguin, 1986). In addition, they imply that attitude toward capital punishment may also predict sentences in non capital and perhaps even non criminal cases. People with a positive attitude toward capital punishment might be harsher than those with a negative attitude in civil lawsuits and in other situations involving punishment (e.g., disciplining children). (1)

The relationship between attitude toward capital punishment and attributions was also investigated because it was speculated that people with a positive attitude might judge the offender's motives more harshly than people with a negative attitude. That is, people with a positive attitude might see the offence as less justified and the offender more driven to his action than people with a negative attitude. As in previous research, attitude toward capital punishment might also be related to perceived intention (Goodman-Delahunty, et al., 1998). It was found that people with a positive attitude toward capital punishment did perceive the murder as more intended than people with a negative attitude. . . . However, there was no relationship between attitude toward capital punishment and the offender being driven. Furthermore, people with a positive attitude perceived the offender as more justified than people with a negative attitude. This was a surprise, because it had been expected that people with a positive attitude would perceive the offender as less justified. Despite the present perception, people with a positive attitude were more punitive than those with a negative attitude. This pattern of results contrasts with the effect of crime on perceived justification and on punishment. The offender was perceived as more justified in the killing circumstances than in the job circumstances and the capital and non capital recommendations were less harsh in the killing circumstances than in the job circumstances. . . .

What, then, is the basis of the present relationship between attitude toward capital punishment and sentencing? The finding that people with a positive attitude to capital punishment were harsher in their capital recommendations than people with a negative attitude is consistent with the theoretical suggestion that attitudes are more likely to predict behavior if they share the same level of specificity (Newcomb, et al., 1992). However, this does not account for the relationship between attitude toward capital punishment and non capital recommendations, which is more consistent with the proposal that belief in the death penalty reflects other personality traits or values (Eysenck, 1954; Stack, 2000). Although these factors were not measured here, it has been found that attitude toward capital punishment is associated with authoritarianism and conservatism (Ray, 1982; Stack, 2000; Vidmar, 1974), and that both of them are associated with harsher punishment (Davis, et al., 1993; Vidmar, 1974). It would be interesting to investigate these variables simultaneously in future research.

Although of secondary interest, sex of the person judging was also investigated as a possible extralegal factor in sentencing recommendations. Sex of participant was significant in [one kind of] analysis, suggesting that women were generally harsher than men. In [another kind of] analysis, it was not significant for the capital recommendation and was only marginally significant for the non capital recommendations. However, with the capital recommendation as a covariate, women were found to deliver harsher non capital recommendations than men. Together with the fact that men and women did not score significantly differently on the Questionnaire on Capital Punishment (QCP), these results contradict previous research showing that men are more likely to recommend the death penalty than women (Honeyman & Ogloff, 1996). The present finding that women were harsher on non capital recommendations has been reported previously (McNamara, et al., 1993), but others have found than men were harsher (McKelvie, 2002) or that there was no sex difference (McKelvie, et al., 1993; Riedel, 1993). Clearly, more work needs to be done to determine the conditions under which sex differences do and do not occur. . . .

Periodical Bibliography

Angus Reid
Global Monitor

"Australians Reject Death Penalty for Murder Cases," October 22, 2007. www.angus-reid.com.

Angus Reid
Global Monitor

"Half of Britons Would Reinstate Death Penalty," March 12, 2008. www.angus-reid.com.

Angus Reid
Global Monitor

"Mexicans Want Death Penalty for Some Crimes," August 20, 2008. www.angus-reid.com.

Angus Reid
Global Monitor

"Palestinian Majority Opposes Death Penalty," October 3, 2008. www.angus-reid.com.

Angus Reid
Global Monitor

"South Koreans Support Death Penalty," March 4, 2009. www.angus-reid.com.

Antoaneta Bezlova

"China: Will the People Choose the Death Penalty?" *IPS Online*, June 14, 2008. www.ips.org.

Robert Buddan

"The Penalty of Death," *Jamaica Gleaner Online*, February 24, 2008. www.jamaica-gleaner.com.

James D. Davidson

"What Catholics Believe About Abortion and the Death Penalty," *National Catholic Reporter*, September 30, 2005.

Bae Hyun-jung

"Killer Reignites Death Row Debate," *Korea Herald*, February 3, 2009.

Telesphor
Remigius Magobe

"Tanzania May Retain Capital Punishment Despite Human Rights' Pressure to Abolish It," *Ground Report Online*, May 23, 2008. www.groundreport.com.

Kenneth Mulligan

"Pope John Paul II and Catholic Opinion Toward the Death Penalty and Abortion," *Social Science Quarterly*, September 1, 2006.

Moyiga Nduru

"Death Penalty: Calls for the Return of Capital Punishment in South Africa," *IPS Online*, June 7, 2006. www.ips.org.

GLOBALVIEWPOINTS

CHAPTER 3

Capital Punishment and Justice

Iran Must Stop Executing Children

Human Rights Watch

Human Rights Watch is a global, nonprofit, nongovernmental human rights organization. In the following viewpoint, Human Rights Watch argues that Iran violates international law and its own legal system by executing juveniles. Though Iran claims to be working to end executions of juveniles, Human Rights Watch argues that the proposed reforms still give judges the option to execute juveniles, and the cases move too slowly through the legal system. Human Rights Watch insists that Iran immediately abolish the execution of juveniles.

As you read, consider the following questions:

1. According to Human Rights Watch, why do the death sentences of juveniles violate Iranian law in some cases?

2. What are qisas crimes?

3. What two international treaties prohibit the imposition of the death penalty on juveniles?

Iran should immediately suspend the use of the death penalty for crimes committed by children under age 18, Human Rights Watch said today. Iran is known to have executed at least 17 juvenile offenders since the beginning of 2004— eight times more than any other country in the world.

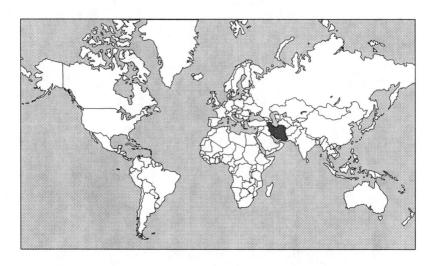

Executing Juveniles Violates the Law

Iran's highest judicial authorities have repeatedly upheld death sentences handed down to juvenile offenders charged with committing crimes when they were as young as 15. Such sentences violate Iran's international treaty obligations, which prohibit the death penalty for crimes committed by people under 18. In some cases, the death sentences also violate Iranian domestic law requiring that children under 18 be tried before special juvenile courts.

"Iran holds the deplorable distinction of leading the world in juvenile executions, and the authorities should end this practice at once," said Clarisa Bencomo, children's rights researcher on the Middle East at Human Rights Watch. "The Iranian government needs to stop sending children to the gallows and start living up to its international obligations by issuing clear legislation to ban the juvenile death penalty."

Iran is known to have executed two juvenile offenders already this year. Syed Mohammad Reza Mousavi Shirazi [hereafter known as Mousavi], 20, was executed in Adel Abd prison in the city of Shiraz on April 22 [2007] for a murder he alleg-

Article 37 of the *Convention on the Rights of the Child,* Which Entered into International Law in 1990

States Parties shall ensure that:

(a) No child shall be subjected to torture or other cruel, inhuman or degrading treatment or punishment. Neither capital punishment nor life imprisonment without possibility of release shall be imposed for offences committed by persons below eighteen years of age;

(b) No child shall be deprived of his or her liberty unlawfully or arbitrarily. The arrest, detention or imprisonment of a child shall be in conformity with the law and shall be used only as a measure of last resort and for the shortest appropriate period of time;

(c) Every child deprived of liberty shall be treated with humanity and respect for the inherent dignity of the human person, and in a manner which takes into account the needs of persons of his or her age. In particular, every child deprived of liberty shall be separated from adults unless it is considered in the child's best interest not to do so and shall have the right to maintain contact with his or her family through correspondence and visits, save in exceptional circumstances;

(d) Every child deprived of his or her liberty shall have the right to prompt access to legal and other appropriate assistance, as well as the right to challenge the legality of the deprivation of his or her liberty before a court or other competent, independent and impartial authority, and to a prompt decision on any such action.

Office of the High Commissioner for Human Rights,
"Convention on the Rights of the Child,"
September 1990. www.unhcr.ch.

edly committed when he was 16. His family was not notified of the planned execution and did not see him prior to the execution.

Documents in Human Rights Watch's possession show that both the lower court and the Supreme Court acknowledged that Mousavi was wrongly tried in an adult court. Nevertheless, the Supreme Court rejected Mousavi's request for a retrial before a juvenile court, accepting the lower court's argument that it was in effect "acting in place of a juvenile court." The Supreme Court confirmed the death sentence, stating "in the light of the direct confession of the accused and the rest of the evidence presented against him, the court sees no significant flaws or shortcomings in the proceedings." Torture and ill-treatment are common in Iranian detention centers, making the court's willingness to accept a child's confession in a death penalty case particularly disturbing.

In a separate case, Iranian authorities executed 17-year-old Sa'id Qanbar Zahi in Zahedan on May 27 [2007]. According to press accounts, Zahi's arrest, confession, trial, sentencing, and execution took place in the space of a few weeks. If true, these factors raise serious doubts that the 17-year-old was able to mount a meaningful defense, and raise further serious concerns about whether other basic fair trial standards were met.

"Torture and ill-treatment are common in Iranian detention centers, making the court's willingness to accept a child's confession in a death penalty case particularly disturbing."

Iran Must Move More Quickly to End Child Executions

Iranian officials have repeatedly stated that they are working to comply with Iran's legal obligations by ending executions of child offenders. High-ranking Judiciary officials have repeatedly said that no juvenile executions take place in Iran. On October 1 [2006], the chief of Tehran's Judiciary, Alireza Avaii, told reporters that "our current policy is that execution sentences for juveniles not be implemented and it has been a long time that any such executions have taken place."

Iranian officials also point to legislation that would establish a new legal framework for juvenile courts, pending in Parliament since July 2006, and claim that it would end executions of juvenile offenders. In fact, this legislation would only offer the possibility of reducing sentences if the judge finds that the defendant is not mentally mature. The proposed legislation (Article 33) makes clear that reduction of sentences in qisas and hadd crimes, for which punishment includes execution, shall be applied "when the complete mental maturity of the defendant is in doubt." Qisas crimes are offenses against a private right where the victim is entitled to a similar retribution, and hadd crimes are offenses with punishments specified under the Islamic penal code.

Article 31.3 of the proposed law would allow a sentence of the death penalty or life imprisonment, if imposed on juvenile defendants ages 15 to 18, to be reduced to a term of imprisonment ranging from two to eight years in a juvenile correctional facility. The majority of juvenile executions in Iran are for qisas and hadd crimes, where judges would continue to have discretion to order executions, if the mental maturity of the defendant is determined by the judge not to be in doubt.

"Only Iran, Sudan, China and Pakistan are known to have executed juvenile offenders since 2004."

"Iran has had more than enough time to demonstrate its commitment to ending the juvenile death penalty," Bencomo said. "The government now needs to take urgent, concrete steps to end this practice."

Human Rights Watch called on the Iranian Parliament to remove from the proposed law the discretion for a judge to impose the death sentence on a juvenile offender. Parliament should also pass the remainder of the proposed legislation mandating reduction of sentences as soon as possible. Human Rights Watch also urged the Council of Guardians, a clerical body with veto power over adopted legislation, not to oppose the proposed legislation.

Only a Few Countries Execute Juveniles

Only Iran, Sudan, China and Pakistan are known to have executed juvenile offenders since 2004. Sudan carried out two such executions in 2005, while China executed one juvenile offender in 2004 and Pakistan executed one juvenile offender in 2006. In contrast, Iran is known to have executed at least three juvenile offenders in 2004, eight in 2005, and four in 2006. In total numbers, only China carries out more executions than Iran. On a per capita basis, Iran executes more people annually than any other country.

Two core international human rights treaties, the Convention on the Rights of the Child and the International Covenant on Civil and Political Rights, prohibit the imposition of the death penalty for crimes committed before the age of 18. Iran has ratified both treaties.

Saudi Arabia's Death Penalty Process Is Arbitrary and Unjust

Christoph Wilcke

Christoph Wilcke is a Saudi Arabian researcher at Human Rights Watch. In the following viewpoint, he states that Saudi Arabia has no established penal code. Instead, judges decide cases based on their personal interpretation of religious teachings. As a result, Wilcke argues that Saudi Arabian courts are arbitrary and unfair. Given the state of Saudi Arabia's legal system, Wilcke maintains that the death penalty should be banned. Wilcke also says Saudi Arabia should cease executing juveniles in contravention of international law.

As you read, consider the following questions:

1. According to Christoph Wilcke, in December 2007, why did a Saudi Arabian court determine that policemen were not guilty of kicking a man to death?

2. According to Wilcke, how many countries retain the death penalty for juveniles?

3. According to Wilcke, what method is used most to carry out executions in Saudi Arabia?

Abdullah al-Shammari was scheduled to be executed shortly after this month's [December 2008] Eid al-Adha, the Muslim Holiday of the Sacrifice, but King Abdullah of Saudi Ara-

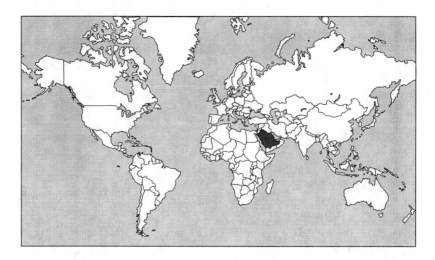

bia decided to grant him a reprieve and study his case. This is welcome, but King Abdullah should not only halt al-Shammari's execution. He should abolish the death penalty in his kingdom.

A System Based on Personal Interpretation

Many nations have abolished capital punishment, recognising its inherent cruelty and finality. Some nations that still have such sentences have strict legal rules and precedents for their use. But in Saudi Arabia, trials are often unfair, and sentences are based on judges' personal interpretations of religious teachings rather than on law. The nation has no penal code, no formal definitions of what constitutes a crime, and no tradition of following established legal precedent. It is also one of the very few countries that continue to execute juveniles.

On the issue of equal justice and legal standards, al-Shammari's conviction is a case in point. The courts found that he killed another man in a fight in Ha'il in 1983, hitting the man on his head with a metal object. A decade later, he was found guilty of "quasi-intentional murder" and ordered to pay blood money. He paid, was freed, married, and fathered children. However, a review court objected and a new set of judges then ruled the murder "intentional," confirming head injuries as the cause, and condemned him to death.

In another case in Saudi Arabia, the religious police beat and kicked a man until he died. A coroner found the cause of death to be a blow to the head. But in late December 2007, a court found the policemen not guilty saying that under the Hanbali tradition of Islamic law a person could not suffer a fatal injury to the head.

"... judges in Quraiyat convicted Fawza Falih of witch-craft in April 2006, based on evidence such as substances found in her jars and the claims of a man who said he became impotent from her spell."

In a third case based on interpretations of religious man-dates, judges in Quraiyat convicted Fawza Falih of witchcraft in April 2006, based on evidence such as substances found in her jars and the claims of a man who said he became impo-tent from her spell. The judges, who sentenced her to death, reached their conclusion not on Qur'anic verses or even ex-amples of the Prophet Muhammad, but quoted unspecified actions of unspecified companions of the Prophet.

Saudi Trials Are Unfair

Saudi trials often violate the most fundamental standards of fairness. Two young men, Muhammad Kuhail, a Canadian, and Muhanna Sa'd, a Jordanian, were sentenced to death in Jeddah for "intentionally killing" another youth in a school-yard brawl in 2007. A blow to the stomach had caused inter-nal bleeding, leading to death from a pre-existing heart condi-tion. The trial judges barred the lawyer for one of the men from attending court sessions and from presenting several de-fence witnesses and cross-examining prosecution witnesses. But a review court still affirmed the verdict.

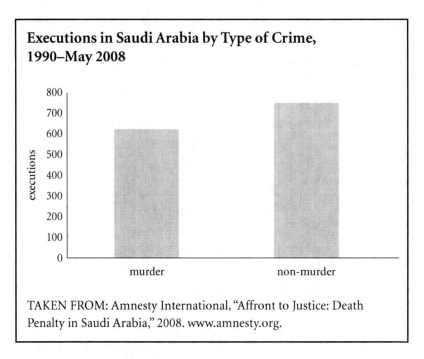

Executions in Saudi Arabia by Type of Crime, 1990–May 2008

TAKEN FROM: Amnesty International, "Affront to Justice: Death Penalty in Saudi Arabia," 2008. www.amnesty.org.

The review court judges conceded that the youth who died and his companions started the fight and that witnesses contradicted one another. Nevertheless, the judges vaguely invoked the writings of a 13th century Islamic scholar to sentence the men to death for "intentional killing," saying that "ignorance of an illness" is no excuse.

Sultan Kuhail, Muhammad's Canadian brother, who was 16 years old at the time of the fight, now faces a possible death penalty in the case because the review court ordered him retried in an adult court after a juvenile court had sentenced him to one year in prison and 200 lashes for his role in the brawl.

The Death Penalty Is Not Administered Justly

Saudi Arabia is among only five countries that retain the death penalty for juveniles in contravention of the Convention on the Rights of the Child, to which the kingdom is a party.

In July 2007, a 16-year-old was executed for a crime he allegedly committed when he was 13. In June 2007, a court sentenced [a] 17-year-old Sri Lankan domestic worker to death after a four-month-old infant in her care choked to death. Saudi Arabia's Shura Council, an appointed parliament, recently passed a law to raise the age of majority from puberty to 18. But even if it is ratified, the consequences for the criminal justice system remain unclear.

Saudi Arabia has executed at least 92 persons so far in 2008, most by public beheadings without warning to them or their families. Two recent beheadings were for dealing amphetamines, which is not among the severe crimes for which international law still permits the death penalty. The government would do well to take a hard look at whether the death penalty is just and whether it actually reduces crime or serves justice for victims of crime.

The Death Penalty in the Palestinian Territories Is Unconstitutional and Unjust

Palestinian Centre for Human Rights

The Palestinian Centre for Human Rights (PCHR) is a nongovernmental organization (NGO) based in Gaza City, dedicated to protecting human rights and upholding democratic principles in the Occupied Palestinian Territory. In this viewpoint, PCHR argues that the judicial code being used in the Palestinian National Authority (PNA) is unconstitutional and violates international law. PCHR calls for the adoption of a new constitutional penal code that abolishes the death penalty in accord with international human rights.

As you read, consider the following questions:

1. Of what crime did the bill of indictment accuse Ayman Ahmed 'Awwad Daghamgha?

2. Are most of the death sentences in the Palestinian territory issued by civilian or military courts?

3. Who must ratify death sentences in the PNA controlled areas?

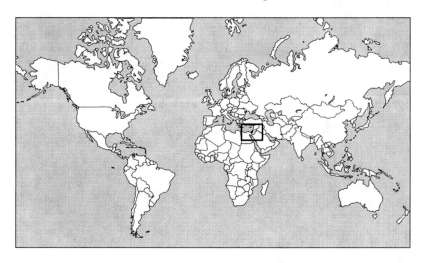

On Wednesday, 12 November 2008, the Military Court in Bethlehem sentenced Ayman Ahmed 'Awwad Daghamgha, 24, a member of the Palestinian General Intelligence Service, from al-Arroub refugee camp north of Hebron, to death by firing squad. The trial was administered by a panel of 3 judges (Chief Justice Fares Douda; Judge Fadi Hijazi; and Judge Ahmed Jaddou'). It was held in the headquarters of the Military Court in Bethlehem. Representatives of the prosecution, Major Ibrahim Abu Saleh and First Lieutenant Akram 'Arar, and the defendant's lawyer, Khalil al-Heeh, were present in the trial.

The court convicted Daghamgha of treason in violation of article 131/A of the Palestinian Revolutionary Penal Code of 1979, and sentenced him in consensus to death, a sentence that needs the Palestinian President's approval and which can be appealed against. The bill of indictment presented against the defendant states that he started to collaborate with the Israeli intelligence service when he was working in a gas station in "Kfar Etzion" settlement, south of Bethlehem, in 1999. Since then, he had monitored stone throwers and students and provided information to the Israeli intelligence in exchange of little money. Later, he joined the Palestinian Naval

Police in the Palestinian National Authority (PNA) before he moved to the General Intelligence Service. He started to monitor Palestinian resistance cells and to provide information on them to the Israeli intelligence. Such information allowed the Israeli Occupation Forces (IOF) to extrajudicially execute [seek out and kill without trial] Jad 'Atallah Salem and Ahmed Is'haq Hamamda, members of the al-Aqsa Martyrs Brigades (an armed wing of Fatah [a Palestinian political party] movement) on 8 March 2008. He also cooperated with IOF in arresting a number of Palestinians.

The Current Penal Code Is Unconstitutional

It is worth noting that the Revolutionary Penal Code of Palestine Liberation Organization is unconstitutional in the PNA, as it has not been presented to, nor approved by, the legislature. PCHR [Palestinian Centre for Human Rights] has repeatedly called for its abolition as it violates international standards of fair trial and does not include fair and independent mechanisms for appealing against court sentences.

Taking this latest sentence into account, a total of seven death sentences have been issued by Palestinian courts since the beginning of 2008. Two of the sentences have been issued in the Gaza Strip and five in the West Bank. Most of these death sentences have been issued by military courts.

"It is worth noting that the Revolutionary Penal Code of Palestine Liberation Organization is unconstitutional . . . as it has not been presented to, nor approved by, the legislature."

On 24 January, 2008, the Military Court in Gaza sentenced Yasser Sa'id Zanoun, 41, to death. On 6 April, the Military Court in Jenin sentenced Tha'er Mahmoud Ramailat, 23, to death. On 28 April, the Hebron Military Court sentenced

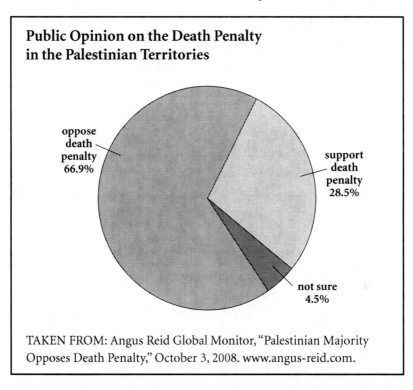

Public Opinion on the Death Penalty in the Palestinian Territories

oppose death penalty 66.9%

support death penalty 28.5%

not sure 4.5%

TAKEN FROM: Angus Reid Global Monitor, "Palestinian Majority Opposes Death Penalty," October 3, 2008. www.angus-reid.com.

'Emad Mahmoud Sa'ed, 25, to death. On 15 July, the Military Court in Jenin sentenced Wa'el Sa'id Sa'ed, 27, and Mohammed Sa'ed Sa'ed, 44, to death. On 20 July, the Military Court in Gaza sentenced thirty-five-year-old Eyad Ahmed Sukkar, 35, from Gaza City, to death.

On 29 October, 2008, the Gaza Court of Cassation, headed by Judge 'Abdul Ra'ouf al-Halabi, Head of the Higher Justice Council, supported the death sentences by hanging issued by the Court of Appeal on 14 June, 2005 against 4 Palestinians. The defendants are: Eihab Diab Abu al-'Amrain, 28; Rami Sa'id Juha, 28; 'Abdul Fattah Mohammed Sammour, 26; and Sa'id Jameel Zuhod, 22.

None of these sentences has yet been carried out, as the implementation of death sentences in the PNA controlled areas requires the Palestinian President's ratification according to the Palestinian Basic Law.

A Just Penal Code Is Needed

PCHR is extremely concerned over the continued application of the death penalty in the PNA controlled areas, and therefore:

1. Calls upon the PNA to announce an immediate moratorium on the use of this form of punishment, which violates international human rights standards and instruments, especially the Universal Declaration of Human Rights (1948), the [International] Covenant on Civil and Political Rights (1966), and the UN Convention Against Torture (1984).

2. Calls upon Palestinian President Mahmoud Abbas not to ratify these cruel and inhumane sentences, and to prevent their implementation.

3. Reiterates that abolishing the death penalty does [not] imply leniency towards dangerous criminals, who must be subjected to punishment that acts as a deterrent, but also maintains human dignity.

4. Calls upon the PNA to review all legislation relative to the death penalty, especially Law No. 74 (1936) that remains effective in the Gaza Strip, and the Jordanian Penal Code No. 16 (1960) that remains effective in the West Bank, and to enact a unified penal code that conforms to the spirit of international human rights instruments, especially those pertaining to the abolition of the death penalty.

Japan's Death Penalty Process Is Shrouded in Secrecy

Charles Lane

Charles Lane is a staff writer at The Washington Post. *In the following viewpoint, Lane notes that Japanese executions are kept secret. Even condemned prisoners are not told when they will die—a practice which some suggest is a form of psychological torture. Lane also says that few safeguards exist to protect accused criminals when they are taken into custody. Japanese executions are also on the rise. Lane notes that human rights organizations have protested, but the Japanese strongly support executions.*

As you read, consider the following questions:

1. According to Charles Lane, how do the names of those executed in Japan leak to the public?
2. What is the minimum hanging period prescribed by law in Japan?
3. According to Lane, why don't anti-death penalty forces want to start a debate about hanging as a method of execution?

Tamaki Mitsui was a bit surprised one Friday when his boss gave him his instructions for the following Monday: to serve as a witness at two hangings. Mitsui, an official of the

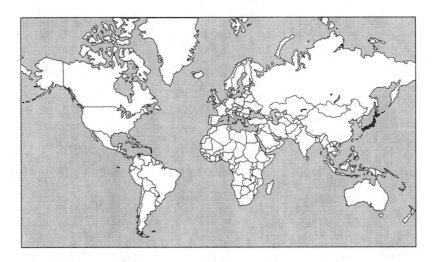

Nagoya High Court Prosecutor's Office, which handles criminal appeals, had argued for the death penalty in three cases himself. He knew that Japanese law requires representatives of the prosecutor's office to witness executions. But he had thought this duty would be assigned by lottery. Still, he accepted it. Part of the job, he thought.

When Monday came, Mitsui took a subordinate with him to the Nagoya Detention Center. It is one of seven Japanese jails where capital offenders await execution—and then go to the gallows. Shortly after 9 o'clock in the morning, Mitsui, his deputy, the director of the detention center, and another prison official sat in a row behind a floor-to-ceiling glass barrier. On the other side of the glass was the death chamber: an empty room, about 18 feet square, with bare white walls and a polished floor of light brown Japanese cypress wood. Dangling from the ceiling, illuminated by floodlights, was a noose. The only sound was the prerecorded chanting of a Buddhist sutra. Mitsui found the setting oddly serene. "It's bizarre to say this, but it was a beautiful place," he recalls, "like a Noh [a form of classic Japanese drama] theater."

Then, a set of double doors on the far side of the execution chamber swung open. The prisoner, escorted by a pair of guards, walked in.

The Death Penalty Is Kept from Public View

It was Nov. 19, 1998, and Tamaki Mitsui was about to see something very few people in the world ever have. In Japan, a high wall of secrecy surrounds the gallows—perhaps only the Imperial Palace is more insulated from public view. No member of the press is allowed to witness hangings. Nor are the families of either the condemned prisoner or his victims. No official descriptions or accounts are published. Executions are not announced until after the fact, and even then official spokespeople say only that they have occurred. (The names of the people hanged leak out from lawyers and family members.) Civil servants ordered to witness executions are required by law to keep silent. Even members of the Diet, Japan's parliament, get no access. When a nine-person delegation from the Diet visited Tokyo's gallows in 2003, it was the first such tour in 30 years. The lawmakers were forbidden to see a hanging or to take photographs.

I spent two months reporting on the death penalty in Japan during the summer of 2004, and Mitsui's was the only eyewitness account of a relatively recent execution I could find. Mitsui, 60, is a trim, slightly nervous man with an officious air—and, it must be acknowledged, a controversial figure in Japan. He was arrested in 2002 on charges of accepting expensive entertainment from gangsters and falsifying a residency certificate in order to obtain an illegal tax break. But the arrest came on the very day he was about to tell a Japanese television program about rampant slush fund abuses in the prosecutor's office. He pleaded not guilty, accusing his former colleagues of a politically motivated prosecution. In February 2005, the Osaka District Court acknowledged that his claims of selective prosecution should be investigated, but nonetheless convicted him on five of six bribery counts. He is free on bail pending his appeal.

Clearly, Mitsui has an ax to grind. And our meeting was arranged by Forum 90, Japan's leading anti-death penalty organization. But his conflict with the Ministry of Justice is unrelated to capital punishment. Although he evinced some ambivalence about what he saw in the gallows, he indicated that he is not an active opponent of the death penalty. His account squared with the few details about the Japanese gallows that have trickled out through other sources. Nobotu Hosaka, a former opposition member of the Diet who joined the delegation that toured the Tokyo gallows in 2003, says the place he and his colleagues visited matches Mitsui's description of the Nagoya death chamber, except that in Tokyo the floor was covered by a carpet. Government officials confirmed certain aspects of Mitsui's description. "On the death penalty, he would seem to have no reason to lie or puff," says David T. Johnson, a professor of sociology at the University of Hawaii who interviewed Mitsui as part of a long-term study of Japan's criminal justice system.

"In Japan, a high wall of secrecy surrounds the gallows—perhaps only the Imperial Palace is more insulated from public view."

Use of the Death Penalty Is on the Rise

Mitsui's story has special relevance now. Not only is Japan the only member of the Group of Seven industrialized countries other than the United States to retain capital punishment, it is also increasing its use of the death penalty. Thanks to declining murder rates and concern over recent death row exonerations, death sentences are on the wane in the United States, reaching 130 in 2004—the lowest number in any year since the United States Supreme Court reinstituted capital punishment in 1976. But, in Japan, the authorities have responded to a recent surge in street crime, and to such events as the 1995 sarin poison gas attack on the Tokyo subway, by seeking more death sentences. The 18 death sentences issued by Japanese trial courts in 2002 were the most in a single year since 1961, when 29 people were sentenced to die. Brushing off criticism from the United Nations Human Rights Commission, the Council of Europe, and Amnesty International, Japanese trial courts sentenced 55 people to death between 2000 and 2003, as many as in the previous 11 years combined. Two men were executed in Japan in 2004, a typical rate for recent years, though two or three times that number is not unusual. This figure is far below the rate in the United States, where 59 people were executed in 2004. But it appears that in the coming years, more and more people will be led to Japan's gallows.

Although the conflict between the United States and Europe over capital punishment is well known, Japan's determined retention of the death penalty shows that the global death penalty debate is not strictly trans-Atlantic. There is also a wide gap between Europe and the democracies—established and emerging—of Asia. Of the Asian countries with freely elected governments, India, Indonesia, the Philippines, South Korea, Sri Lanka, Taiwan, and Thailand all have capital punishment. This list, to be sure, encompasses a range of death penalty policies. Taiwan is in the process of phasing out capital punishment, while in Thailand, a nation of 65 million people, there are almost 1,000 men and women currently under sentence of death, many for drug offenses.

". . . it appears that in the coming years, more and more people will be led to Japan's gallows."

Death Row Inmates Do Not Know When They Will Die

The man stepping through the double doors on that November morning six years ago was 61-year-old Tatsuaki Nishio. In his younger days, he had been a gang leader. Between 1976 and 1977, he committed three crimes in the Nagoya area: He directed a subordinate to strangle a 48-year-old employee of a Nagoya construction company and attempted two other murders. The Supreme Court of Japan denied his last appeal in 1989. On the day of his execution, prison guards awakened him and informed him it was his time to die. In Japan, death row prisoners are not told in advance of their execution dates—a practice international human rights organizations condemn as a form of psychological torment.

But the government argues that the process is compassionate and prudent, insisting that advance notice would create unnecessary anxiety when prisoners should be adjusting to the inevitable. "A death row inmate is every day waiting for death, so it is easily understood that he may easily be emotionally destabilized," says Satoru Ohashi, an assistant director of the Ministry of Justice's Correction Bureau. "And if he becomes emotionally destabilized, he may commit suicide, escape, or harm the prison staff." Additionally, it is said, publicity about individuals on death row would invade the privacy of their families, who feel shamed or ostracized because of their criminal kin.

Death penalty opponents say the Ministry of Justice's real purpose is to break the inmates' will, to discourage extended appeals. "If you have no one to help you and you have access to clergy who say, 'You committed a crime, so accept death,' and you live every day staring at a wall, who wouldn't begin to want to die?" says Yuichi Kaido, a prominent defense lawyer who represents capital defendants. "This kind of treatment induces them to give up retrial petitions." Japanese opponents of the death penalty note that at least some death row inmates, or their families, were given notice of their pending executions until about 30 years ago. According to a 2001 article by Kaido, condemned inmate and murderer Kiyohachi Horikoshi was actually permitted to meet his mother the day before his execution in December 1975. But, a month later, Kiyoshi Ōkubo, another convicted murderer, was executed without warning, and no one else has been given advance notice since then. The timing of the change, opponents argue, shows that it was meant to counteract a 1975 decision by the Supreme Court of Japan that loosened the requirements that death row inmates must meet to win a new trial. The court decision encouraged many new retrial petitions, which were previously rare.

"It seems incredible that confessions are not given to the court as either tapes or verbatim transcripts. Rather, they are rewritten and summarized by the authorities themselves."

Japan's Justice System Invites Abuses

If that was the government's true intent, it did not entirely succeed. The eventual result of the 1975 ruling was the exoneration and release of four men who had been on death row since being convicted of murder and sentenced to death in the decade after World War II—but who had always insisted on their innocence. In each case, there were serious questions about the handling of evidence and the methods authorities used to extract confessions. Perhaps the most notorious such miscarriage of justice involved Sakae Menda, who in 1948, at the age of 23, was convicted of a double ax murder. The conviction was based on the contradiction-riddled testimony of a prostitute and Menda's own confession, extracted after spending 80 hours in a police station without sleep.

The Ministry of Justice tightened its procedures after those cases, which were part of the reason Japan suspended executions for 40 months between November 1989 and March 1993. Yet some problematic aspects of Japan's death penalty system remain essentially unchanged. Perhaps the most basic—the authorities' reliance on confessions—is not unique to capital cases.

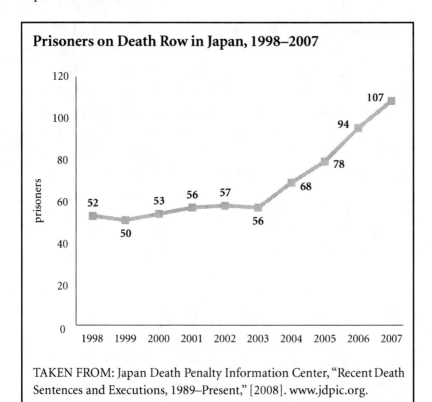

Prisoners on Death Row in Japan, 1998–2007

TAKEN FROM: Japan Death Penalty Information Center, "Recent Death Sentences and Executions, 1989–Present," [2008]. www.jdpic.org.

Traditionally, Japanese courts have treated a defendant's own admissions as more persuasive than other evidence, including circumstantial evidence or even forensics. Although suspects have a theoretical right to remain silent, they may also be held and questioned without access to a lawyer for up to 23 days. Even after they have contacted an attorney, they are not entitled to have counsel present during questioning. As a result, the Japanese criminal justice system has been plagued by allegations of physical and psychological abuse during interrogation. From an American perspective, it seems incredible that confessions are not given to the court as either tapes or verbatim transcripts. Rather, they are rewritten and summarized by the authorities themselves.

A Hanging in Japan

As it happens, there was no serious question of Tatsuaki Nishio's guilt, though the government waited to execute him until he exhausted his legal claims. That is standard Ministry of Justice policy; however, the authorities reserve the right to proceed with an execution if they feel an inmate is simply filing repetitive or baseless appeals. By the time Nishio appeared before Mitsui, he would also have been offered a final meal or some sweets, a cigarette, and a meeting with the clergy of his choice. The government says the condemned may draft a last-minute will, but anti-death penalty campaigners say this is sometimes nothing more than a few words hastily murmured to a guard.

When he stepped through the double doors, Nishio was blindfolded and dressed in a white cotton robe, Mitsui says. His hands were bound behind him. His feet were bare. The guards led him to a square marked in the middle of the floor, directly beneath the noose. One guard placed the noose around his neck. Nishio stood there for a moment, silent, seemingly calm, bathed in lamplight.

Then, without warning, the square beneath Nishio's feet, a trap door, swung open. He dropped straight down. The noose tightened. Nishio's neck snapped, and he stopped moving. His body now hung in a separate room downstairs.

As Nishio dangled there and the minutes dragged by in silence, Mitsui began to grow uneasy. What were they waiting for? Eventually, he turned to the director of the detention center and asked: "Why so long?" Japan's prison law refers to a minimum hanging period of five minutes. But the director replied simply that this was the way things are done. The witnesses returned to their silent vigil.

Finally, after 30 long minutes, the director ordered Mitsui and a prison doctor to go downstairs and examine Nishio. On the lower level, Mitsui noticed that there was no theater-style floor, just bare concrete. With the guards' help, Mitsui and the doctor laid Nishio down and stripped off his robe and blind-fold, in accordance with the prison law, which provides that "the countenance of the dead shall be inspected after hang-ing." They rolled the body back and forth, noting that it was unscathed except for a bruise on Nishio's neck. There was no question: The sentence had been carried out.

"Polls indicate that public support for capital punish-ment is even stronger in Japan than in the United States—more than 81 percent in a February 2005 sur-vey."

Japanese Attitudes Toward Capital Punishment

As I listened to Mitsui, it was clear that he had been made ex-tremely anxious and uncomfortable by that 30-minute wait, for reasons that he could not quite articulate. His disquiet made me wonder what the Japanese public would think if they knew, in detail, what he knows. Toyoko Ogino, an inter-preter I worked with in the coal mining town of Ōmuta, was surprised when I told her that prisoners were hanged. "I thought that was just an expression," she said. Perhaps greater information would make no difference: Polls indicate that public support for capital punishment is even stronger in Ja-pan than in the United States—more than 81 percent in a February 2005 survey.

Nor is the use of hanging as a method of execution con-troversial in Japan. It has been all but abandoned in the United States, in part because of fears it might subject prisoners to unnecessary suffering, especially if the noose fails to work as designed. But, apart from a 1961 decision by the Supreme Court of Japan, which found that hanging does not violate the postwar Japanese Constitution's ban on "cruel" punishment, Japan has not reconsidered a form of execution first adopted by the Meiji-era Grand Council of State in 1873. Mitsui said he was untroubled. "They die instantly," he assured me. "There is no agony."

Indeed, Japan adopted hanging during the Meiji Restoration [in the second half of the 1800s] as a reformist alternative to decapitation. A new debate over hanging does not seem to be in the interest of either the Japanese government or the country's small anti-death penalty movement. The former does not wish to hash out any aspect of the death penalty in public; the latter does not want to appear to accept the death penalty's legitimacy by arguing over how it is carried out.

As Mitsui describes it, the hanging of Nishio seemed to happen all by itself. The man stood on the trap door; the trap door opened; he went down. This was by design. Ordinary prison guards operate the gallows. They may not refuse the job, even if they have a conscientious objection. Officials understand this system can create stress. "As you can imagine, it's a very emotionally demanding task," says Satoru Ohashi of the Correction Bureau. So, Ohashi said, a solution has been found. Five guards press separate buttons simultaneously. Only one of these is the button that actually opens the trap door. And all of this takes place outside the witnesses' field of vision— offstage, as it were. There is a hanging, but no identifiable hangman.

Five guards press separate buttons simultaneously. Only one of these is the button that actually opens the trap door. . . . There is a hanging, but no identifiable hangman.

No One Asks About the Hanging

For Mitsui, it was a long day at the gallows. After Nishio had been hanged, guards brought in Masamichi Ida, 56. Ida used to work for a car repair shop in Aichi Prefecture, near Nagoya.

He took out a life insurance policy on a 20-year-old customer and then, in November 1979, went sailing with the young man and pushed him overboard. He was also convicted of two other murders near Kyoto in 1983. Ida was executed in exactly the same manner as Nishio, Mitsui says—including that excruciating 30-minute wait.

In the early afternoon, Mitsui returned to his office and wrote up a report to the Ministry of Justice in Tokyo, confirming that the prisoners had been duly executed. His office-mates had thoughtfully spread salt on the floor before his return; in Shinto tradition, death is impure, and salt is thought to purify those who have had contact with the dead. But he and his coworkers did not actually discuss what he had seen. His boss gave him the rest of the day off. Returning home, he did not tell his wife about his day, either.

Even now, though, Mitsui muses about the strange beauty of the death chamber, that secret theater of polished floors and tasteful lighting. The condemned man enters blindfolded. "Why do they prepare such a beautiful place, but the prisoner is not able to see?" he wondered in our interview, then answered his own question: "Maybe it is for the benefit of the witnesses—to make them feel calmer."

Singapore's Mandatory Death Penalty Is Unjust

South Asia Human Rights Documentation Center

The South Asia Human Rights Documentation Center (SAHRDC) is a network of individuals across South Asia who investigate, document, and disseminate information about human rights. In the following viewpoint, SAHRDC argues that Singapore's mandatory death sentence for drug offenses violates international human rights standards. It also violates the Constitution of Singapore, since it takes judicial sentencing powers from the courts and gives them to the legislature. Singapore's government defends the mandatory death penalty as necessary to keep crime rates low. According to SAHRDC, it also restricts debate on the subject.

As you read, consider the following questions:

1. What was the nationality of Van Tuong Nguyen [also known as Nguyen Tuong Van], who was executed for drug trafficking in Singapore in 2005?

2. Why did a Singaporean Royal Commission investigating a proposal to permit judicial discretion conclude that sentences should be mandatory?

South Asia Human Rights Documentation Center, "No Justification for Mandatory Death Penalty," Human Rights Features, January 31, 2006. Copyright © SAHRDC. Reproduced by permission.

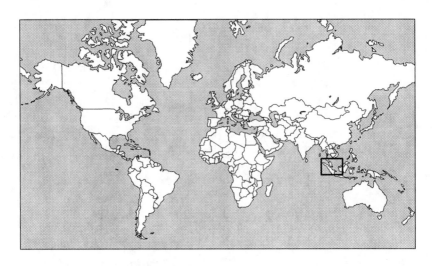

3. In an interview with the BBC [British Broadcasting Corporation] in 2001, what did premier Goh Chok Tong say when asked how many executions had occurred in Singapore?

Singapore, though enjoying a reputation of being wealthy and progressive, falls significantly short when it comes to compliance with international human rights standards. The execution [in 2005] of an Australian, 25-year-old Van Tuong Nguyen [also known as Nguyen Tuong Van], for trafficking 396 grams of heroin attracted widespread condemnation of Singapore's notorious mandatory death penalty, and rightly so. In a statement, the UN Special Rapporteur on extrajudicial, summary or arbitrary executions, Professor Philip Alston, said that "making such a penalty mandatory—thereby eliminating the discretion of the court—makes it impossible to take into account mitigating or extenuating circumstances and eliminates any individual determination of an appropriate sentence in a particular case".

Singapore is believed to have the highest per capita execution rate in the world and has executed more than 400 people since 1991, 70 percent of which are reportedly for drug offences.

Under the Misuse of Drugs Act (MDA), judges must administer the death penalty to any person trafficking more than 15 grams of heroin and may not consider any extenuating circumstances or mitigating factors in a particular case.

Nguyen's case, it is hoped, will impress upon the international community the need to closely scrutinise Singapore's human rights record, and critique it where necessary. Singapore's glittering prosperity conceals a number of horrifying abuses, and it is time the international community took note of some of these concerns.

The Mandatory Death Penalty Is Illegal

Professor Alston echoed the concerns of many lawyers and activists when he argued that the mandatory penalty denies the judiciary the necessary discretion to sentence fairly and appropriately.

He referred to the authority of a number of international cases which have found that the mandatory penalty is in violation of the international prohibition on cruel, inhuman or degrading treatment or punishment. He said that in Nguyen's case, the Court of Appeal failed to make a thorough examination of prior Privy Council decisions. One case conspicuously absent from the Court's deliberations was *Boyce and Joseph v. The Queen*, decided in 2004, in which four of the Law Lords endorsed the statement that "[n]o international human rights tribunal anywhere in the world has ever found a mandatory death penalty regime compatible with international human rights norms."

In Nguyen's case, Singapore upheld the validity of the mandatory death penalty, relying primarily on the precedent in *Ong Ah Chuan v. Public Prosecutor*, where the penalty was found to be not unusual according to international practice. As Alston points out, however, this decision has been superceded by subsequent cases such as *Reyes v. The Queen* where Lord Bingham commented that "[t]he decision in [*Ong Ah*

Chuan v. Public Prosecutor] was made at a time when international jurisprudence on human rights was rudimentary."

The Court of Appeal also insisted that "the mandatory death sentence prescribed under the MDA is sufficiently discriminating to obviate any inhumanity in its operation." However, as Professor Alston points out, "discrimination" only occurs within the act and the courts have no capacity to discriminate in the sense referred to by the recent Privy Council decisions. The legislature has effectively usurped the judges' legitimate role to exercise discretion in determining a just sentence.

Nguyen's case also illuminates the fact that Singapore's mandatory death penalty undermines not only international principles, but also domestic constitutional provisions.

Nguyen argued that the penalty . . . breached Articles 9(1) and 93 of the Constitution which assert the fundamental liberty of the person and which assign judicial powers to the courts. The Court of Appeal, however, refused to engage in these arguments. Instead, it made reference to a Privy Council decision from Belize, where the mandatory death penalty was found to contradict Belize's constitutional provision against "torture and inhuman or degrading treatment or punishment." The Court of Appeal concluded that because no such provision existed in Singapore, the mandatory sentencing laws did not amount to a constitutional breach. In saying this, the court was able to avoid consideration of the constitutional validity of the mandatory death penalty. Because the Singaporean judiciary is effectively under the control of the ruling People's Action Party (PAP), any constitutional interpretation contrary to the government's position is virtually impossible.

Singapore Defends Mandatory Death Sentencing

A Singaporean Royal Commission investigating a proposal to permit judicial discretion in imposing the death penalty con-

Singapore Fights for the Death Penalty

Singapore's strong pro-death penalty stand during the November [2007] U.N. General Assembly vote on a draft resolution calling for an end to the death penalty has disappointed many and left Singaporeans asking why the city-state is willing to risk international condemnation to pursue the death penalty so publicly as a solution to crime.

Singapore was one of the few countries that fiercely opposed the moratorium when the vote was taken on Nov 15 with 99 in favour, 52 against and 33 abstentions.

The U.S. and China joined many developing countries, notably from the Islamic world, in voting 'no' after an acrimonious debate.

Baradan Kuppusamy,
"Death Penalty-Singapore: Stand at UN Leaves Many Angered,"
IPS Online, *December 3, 2007. http://ipsnews.net.*

cluded that sentences should preferably be mandatory to prevent burdening judges with such a responsibility. Prominent Singaporean Senior Counsel and former deputy Public Prosecutor K.S. Rajah has argued that the judiciary is made of "sterner stuff" and can capably assign punishments as it sees fit.

The Singaporean government admits that it has "some of the toughest laws in the world such as for drug trafficking and the use of firearms" but defends these by describing the "relatively safe and crime-free environment" and the need to enhance the "attraction of Singapore to tourists and investors." These claims, advanced to excuse the death penalty by reference to low crime rates, still cannot justify the taking of human life. Moreover, there is no supporting research for the claims. According to a report by the NSW [New South Wales] Bureau of Crime Statistics examining 74 studies into the death penalty over a 51-year period, there is no evidence that the death penalty deters potential criminals.

"The Singapore government works hard to prevent open discussions on the death penalty using its infamous laws which restrict the media and outlaw public speeches. . . ."

Singapore Restricts Discussion of Death Penalty

Amnesty International has described official information concerning the use of the death penalty in Singapore as "shrouded in mystery." Precise numbers of the executed are difficult to ascertain. Some figures were provided in answer to a parliamentary question in January 2001. Additional information was released in 2003 following an embarrassing admission by Singapore's former premier, Mr. Goh Chok Tong, during an interview with the BBC [British Broadcasting Corporation] that he was unaware of the number executed because he had "more important issues to worry about." His initial estimate placed the number of executions occurring before October 2003 at 70 or 80. His office later "corrected" this figure as being only 10.

The Singapore government works hard to prevent open discussions on the death penalty using its infamous laws which restrict the media and outlaw public speeches and "unlicensed" gatherings. The press may not give an independent opinion on the executions in Singapore and news of hangings is generally only made public after they have taken place.

In April 2005, the Singaporean government refused to grant a permit to Tim Parritt of Amnesty International to speak at a forum on the death penalty. Singapore Democratic Party leader Chee Soon Juan described the refusal as "a blatant attempt to keep the matter under wraps", noting that Mr. Parritt had effectively been denied "the opportunity to speak and to engage Singaporeans in an open discussion on this life-and-death matter."

The Law Society in Singapore, which includes every practicing lawyer in the country, appears similarly uncomfortable with the penalty. It has recently established a Committee to undertake an independent review of the practice. While the results of such a review may be ignored by the government, it is a clear demonstration of growing public uneasiness about the death penalty in Singapore.

Reforms May Make China's Death Penalty Process More Just

Hong Lu and Terance D. Miethe

Hong Lu and Terance D. Miethe are professors of criminal law at the University of Nevada, Las Vegas. In the following viewpoint, the authors argue that while China is unlikely to abolish the death penalty, judicial reforms may make the punishment less frequent and more just. In particular, the authors explore movements to restrict the number of capital offenses and coerced confessions and to reestablish the Supreme Court as the final review authority in capital cases.

As you read, consider the following questions:

1. In the 1990s, did the scope of capital punishment—the number of crimes punishable by the death penalty—increase or decrease?
2. According to the authors, why is it difficult to curb police coercion even though the law officially prohibits police torture and brutality?
3. According to the authors, what four supporting arguments are used to justify the Supreme Court's reestablishment as the final review authority in death penalty cases?

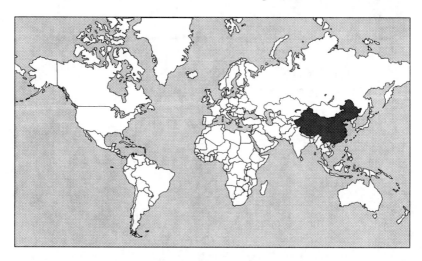

The death penalty is at a major crossroad in contemporary Chinese society. From a historical perspective, its imposition in the current context has become more rational and civilized. However, from a modern global perspective, the Chinese government's desire to become a major player and leader of the international community will inevitably lead to its reassessment of the death penalty practice. Under the current sociopolitical conditions in China, the death penalty seems to have sufficient official and grassroots support to play a continued role in crime control and order maintenance even in the face of a global movement toward its abolition. . . .

Restricting the Scope of the Death Penalty

A series of legal developments . . . [has] been underway to reform many aspects of the legal system in China since the 1990s. . . . Of relevance to the death penalty are reforms of the substantive law (e.g., limiting the scope of capital offenses) and procedural law (e.g., the use of torture, confessions, legal representation, the Supreme Court's final review and approval authority).

While divergent opinions exist on the future direction of the death penalty in China, scholars and practitioners seemed

Lawyers in China Face Government Harassment

If Chinese lawyers now enjoy greater administrative and financial independence from the state, legal restrictions still impede their ability to provide an effective defense. . . . Lawyers who have taken politically sensitive cases or sought redress for abuses committed by Party and state agents have consistently faced abuses. . . .

Such disincentives, combined with pervasive political control of the judiciary, effectively deter China's legal profession at large from engaging in work that is perceived by Party and government authorities as a threat or as a potential source of embarrassment. These dynamics undermine citizens' ability to exercise their legal rights and exacerbate rising levels of social unrest, as citizens are denied meaningful legal avenues to seek redress for abuses.

Instances of abuse by the national government or local authorities against lawyers have disproportionately affected the small group of influential lawyers who are part of the *weiquan*, or "rights protection" movement. Weiquan lawyers represent on cases involving some of the most serious human rights issues that beset China today: rural land confiscation, unlawful forced eviction, abuse of power, torture and ill-treatment, miscarriage of justice, labor exploitation and discriminatory access of education and health care to migrants.

Human Rights Watch has documented over a dozen cases of lawyers who have been threatened, assaulted, detained and suspended by the authorities in retaliation for their work as human rights defenders.

Human Rights Watch, "China UPR Submission,"
September 30, 2008. www.hrw.org.

to converge on the need to restrict the scope of capital offenses. . . . The current 1997 criminal law stipulated a total of 68 capital offenses, encompassing broad categories of violent, property, public safety, public order, economic, and corruption offenses. This dramatic expansion of the scope of capital offenses in the 1990s contradicted the global trend of the restrictive use of capital punishment, and was inconsistent with the Chinese legal reforms of professionalism, formalism, and humanism.

[Scholar Xingliang] Chen laid out convincing arguments on the feasibility of limiting the scope of capital offenses in contemporary China. He pointed out that among the total of sixty-eight current capital offenses, about one-third of the capital offenses have never been used in practice; and another one-third of these capital crimes consisted of nonviolent, nonlethal offenses (e.g., corruption, economic offenses, and public order offenses). Following international practices, if these nonviolent and nonlethal offenses could be sanctioned with non-capital punishment (e.g., long-term incarceration and severe economic penalties), the number of capital offenses could be substantially reduced to around twenty.

". . . among the total of sixty-eight current capital offenses, about one-third of the capital offenses have never been used in practice; and another one-third . . . consisted of nonviolent, nonlethal offenses."

The major obstacle to the abolition of capital punishment for economic and corruption offenses is the law's apparent deterrence effect. In particular, given the current sociopolitical context, many fear that offenders convicted of economic and corruption crimes (e.g., smuggling and graft) will easily get away with the crime if a non-capital punishment is imposed because of the rampant political and judicial corruption.

Other scholars have argued that restricting the scope of the death penalty also required that ad hoc interpretations and amendments issued by the National People's Congress [NPC, China's legislative body] and other governmental agencies should be eliminated. By abolishing these practices, a primary means of expanding the scope of the death penalty and implementing mandatory punishments in some cases (e.g., corruption) is severely restricted.

Increasing Defendants' Rights

One of the major challenges in curbing erroneous death sentences and executions involves the role of torture and coerced confessions. Even though the 1996 revised criminal procedure law stipulated the principle of presumption of innocence and entitled more rights to attorneys to curb police abuse, almost all cases of wrongful convictions and/or executions exposed by the media in recent years involved some forms of physical torture and forced confessions. For example, She Xianglin, a former security guard in Hubei province, spent eleven years in jail for murdering his wife. He was released in April 2005 after his wife reappeared in the village. She told reporters that he was tortured by the police interrogators, deprived of sleep for ten days and forced to leave his finger mark on the documents that stated that (1) he admitted to the killing of his wife and (2) the body discovered, which was unidentifiable, was his wife's. In another case involving rape and murder in Hebei, a twenty-one-year-old man was recently found to have been wrongfully executed in 1994 for a crime he did not commit. His attorney recalled that the defendant said that he was beaten prior to confessing the crime.

Holding suspects for prolonged custody and collecting evidence by torture is especially prevalent in rural areas where legal training is lacking among the legal professionals and traditional views and methods of brutality and abuse are more tolerated. According to Chief Justice Xiao Yang's work report to NPC sessions, 80 percent of lawsuits on police torture nationwide were filed at courts of the grassroots level (e.g., rural areas and urban districts).

"Reforms to curb torture and forced confessions have been placed on the top agenda of several agencies."

The widespread police interrogation practices of torture and coercion to extract confession, while having its deep historical roots, reflect more of the weaknesses in the current legal system. For example, the current law does afford a defendant's rights to remain silent and adequate legal representation. Though the law prohibits police torture and brutality, it does not provide mechanisms to ensure its enforcement (e.g., no exclusionary rules; rare and lenient disposition on violators, overemphasis on confession evidence). Any legal safeguards are further restricted because defense attorneys are not allowed to be present in critical stages of the initial criminal investigation before suspects/defendants make their confessions.

Reforms to curb torture and forced confessions have been placed on the top agenda of several agencies. For example, the procuratorate in China is in charge of supervising the police and judicial activities. It bears the direct responsibility and authority to regulate, monitor, and investigate police misconduct in torture and forced confessions. A report showed that the procuratorate in 2004 had probed and dealt with more than seven hundred cases involving illegal police detention and torture nationwide and an approximately 1,600 police officers were charged with abuse power.

Preventing Forced Confessions

Internally, the procuratorate attempts to strictly follow the agency protocol to detect and investigate any allegations by criminal defendants of the possible claims of confessions extracted by torture. The top official of the Supreme People's Procuratorate (SPP) told a reporter that in the future, before prosecuting a case, criminal suspects will be asked whether they were forced to make a false confession, and the lead prosecutor must carefully examine reports prepared by the police to detect any signs of forced confessions. Once determined, prosecutors must immediately report the police abuse to the higher level of the procuratorate and ask the police to rectify the problem. For serious abuse, the police will be investigated and held legally responsible.

Recognizing that forced confession is a "salient problem" in the criminal justice system, the legislative body is likely to amend a bill on Offenses against Public Order, aiming at increasing criminal penalty for the violation of public order and limiting police power. This bill is expected to stipulate in more stern language that forced confessions are "strictly forbidden and legally invalid." Police officers who are involved in extorting confessions through torture will be held either criminally or administratively responsible based on the severity of their conduct.

While it is important for the oversight judicial and procuratorate agencies to be more alert of police misconduct, it seems more effective to simply reform the process of police interrogations. A recent report from the Ministry of Public Security suggests that China will gradually adopt live voice recording of the entire police interrogation involving lethal cases and organized crime cases. Another pilot project led by the top prosecution offices and the Chinese University of Political Science and Law was recently launched to allow suspects to be interrogated in the presence of lawyers, or by recording and videotaping the entire process. Other reform attempts included allowing defense attorneys greater access to police and prosecution files, increasing their presence during police interrogation at all times, and improving and enforcing the State Compensation Law that was passed in 1995. The State Compensation Law mainly affords plaintiffs' rights to seek financial compensation from the government when affected by wrongful and illegal administrative decisions and measures (e.g., police coercion and torture).

"A recent report from the Ministry of Public Security suggests that China will gradually adopt live voice recording of the entire police interrogation involving lethal cases. . . ."

Standardizing Supreme Court Review

According to several speeches in 2004 and 2005 by Xiao Yang (President of the Supreme Court), China's Supreme Court is contemplating whether to take back the final review and approval authority for the death penalty in all cases. [Currently the death penalty for some crimes such as murder, robbery, rape, and arson can be approved by superior courts in local jurisdictions.] Premiere Wen in 2005 also stated that one of the judicial reforms will include the recall of the final review and approval authority by the Supreme Court. Recently, legal scholars and lawmakers have urged the Supreme Court to take back the final review and approval authority on all death penalty cases. All of these officials', scholars' and practitioners' comments and activities indicate that the use of the Supreme Court as the only final authority over capital cases will become inevitable in the near future in China.

The current debate on the final review and approval of the death penalty cases has converged on the need for a central, national authority for this function. However, different groups diverge on their views about how the system will be set up. More specifically, the debate focuses on the goals, the nature of the review and approval process, and the organizational structure.

Competing theories and justifications have been advanced to support the Supreme Court's reestablishment as the final review and approval authority on the death penalty cases. Some of these supporting arguments include (1) preventing erroneous killings, (2) reducing the use of death sentences, (3) providing uniform standards for death sentences, and (4) serving the symbolic function that the Chinese government is cautious when meting out the death sentence.

Different goals of capital punishment may place different demands on financial resources and professional expertise on the Supreme Court. For example, if the goal is serving as a symbolic function to show the world that all death sentences are finally reviewed and approved by the Supreme Court in China, it may only mean an additional administrative layer that capital cases must go through, rather than involving any substantive review of either the facts or evidence in the process. In this regard, other goals such as preventing erroneous killing and limiting the use of death sentences may not be fulfilled. In contrast, if the main goal is to unify the standards and limiting the scope of capital punishment, the Supreme Court must more carefully review the facts and the laws in the case, which requires more resources and experienced judicial officers in this area.

Possible Processes for Supreme Court Review

Two different processes have been proposed for the final review and approval authority on the death penalty. One involves administrative review. This administrative review refers to the process of review that focuses primarily on procedural justice. Under this perspective, if the application of the law was correct and no obvious illegal conduct was involved (e.g., coerced confessions, erroneous judgments), the lower court's ruling should be sustained. This type of review is driven by formality and process, involves little witness testimony in court, no public hearings, and focuses primarily on documents prepared by procuratorate, the defense, and the lower courts. Under this model of administrative review, the scope of the review is quite limited and the symbolic function is greater than its actual value of preventing possible errors in judgment.

The other process for the final review and approval authority involves an adjudicative component. This adjudicative process is similar to a normal trial. Facts, evidence, and the application of law must be reviewed more closely and carefully. It involves necessary hearings and testimonies from both sides, particularly from the condemned offender and the defense attorney. The advantage of this adjudicative process certainly is the reexamination of facts and evidence and possible prevention of any erroneous facts and evidence admitted to the court. Its drawback is that it demands more resources.

Scholars and legal practitioners have also debated about how to set up the organizational structure for the final review and approval of capital cases. Three views emerged: (1) to set up regional district courts (e.g., similar to the U.S. federal district courts); (2) to set up circuit courts; and (3) to entrust the Supreme Court, headquartered in Beijing, to review and approve all cases. Generally speaking, legal practitioners preferred the Supreme Court to be the only and final authority over the review and approval of all capital cases because it requires little organizational restructure and prevents local protectionism and corruption. In contrast, scholars seemed to be more in favor of setting up circuit courts in each province for the following reasons. Circuit courts can significantly reduce financial costs associated with the increasing number of capital cases reviewed by the Supreme Court by cutting down the costs for transporting and providing accommodations for defendants, witnesses and legal professionals from one province to the capital city of Beijing for live hearings. Circuit courts could also prevent local protectionism and corruption from judicial officers and legal personnel appointed by the Supreme

Court and through a rotating work schedule (e.g., judicial officers change their post every few years to prevent [them] from establishing local ties).

Currently, the more pragmatic approach proposed by the legal practitioners seemed to win over other arguments. In fact, the Standing Committee of the National People's Congress announced the creation of the No. 3, No. 4, and No. 5 Criminal Courts within the Supreme Court. Many predict that the creation of these new courts within the Supreme Court will help pave the way for the Court to take back its final review and approval authority over the death penalty cases.

In Russia, a Death Penalty Moratorium May Lead to Abolition

Victoria Sergeyeva and Kester Kenn Klomegah

Victoria Sergeyeva is Penal Reform International's director for Russia, Ukraine, and Belarus. In the following interview with Inter Press Service (IPS) correspondent Kester Kenn Klomegah, Sergeyeva says that Russia has had a moratorium on the death penalty since 1996. Since most Russians and many legislators still support the death penalty, it is unlikely, though not impossible, that the death penalty will be abolished before the moratorium expires in 2010. Sergeyeva argues, however, that life imprisonment in Russia is not necessarily a humane alternative to the death penalty.

As you read, consider the following questions:

1. Does the Russian Constitution bar the death penalty, according to Victoria Sergeyeva?

2. In 1999, the Constitutional Court in Russia said no death penalties could be issued until what conditions were met?

3. According to Sergeyeva, are prison populations world-wide increasing or decreasing?

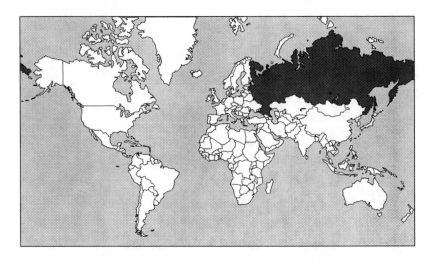

How close is Russia to abolishing the death penalty? Possibly just two or three years away, suggests Penal Reform International's director for Russia, Ukraine and Belarus, Victoria Sergeyeva. In an interview with IPS [Inter Press Service] correspondent Kester Kenn Klomegah, she explains that leading Russian politicians have already made up their minds on the issue, though their fellow MPs [Members of Parliament] still need prodding out of their indecision. Across the country, young, educated city dwellers would welcome the move.

IPS: The Russian Federation recently backed the U.N. General Assembly's call for the world to move towards abolishing the death penalty. What is the legal position today in Russia on capital punishment?

Victoria Sergeyeva (VS): Since 1996, Russia has observed a de facto moratorium on executions. The moratorium came into force by presidential decree at the time the Russian Federation was joining the Council of Europe. Later, Russia also signed—but has yet to ratify—Protocol No. 6 to the European Convention on Human Rights on the abolition of the death penalty. So, since 1996 no death sentences have been handed down or executions carried out. But a final decision on the future of the death penalty still has to be taken. The Russian

Constitution still allows for the possibility of the death penalty. And the Russian Federation's Criminal Code still envisages capital punishment for five categories of crimes.

IPS: Apart from the 1996 presidential decree, has the moratorium been adopted into law?

VS: In 1999, the Constitutional Court did issue an unprecedented ruling on the moratorium—at least a temporary one. It said that no death sentences could be passed down anywhere in the Russian Federation until jury trials had been introduced everywhere in the country. So, this was a constitutional ban on any court issuing death sentences until this was the case.

IPS: You said it was a temporary ban. When do you expect this process of introducing jury trials to be completed?

VS: The . . . [Chechen] Republic [Chechnya] will be the last region to complete this process. In January 2007, the State Duma [the lower legislative house in Russia] approved a law postponing trial by jury there until 2010.

IPS: The ruling on jury trials would, it seems, not stand in the way of abolishing the death penalty ahead of whatever happens in Chechnya. Why has the Russian Federation been so slow in formally abolishing the death penalty?

VS: First of all, there's no common support for death penalty abolition among Russian deputies. Many MPs are in favour of capital punishment. The death penalty has been discussed a few times in the State Duma. But each time the debates have ended fruitlessly.

The authorities have put enormous efforts into ensuring capital punishment is not applied. But there's something preventing them from striking out this punishment from legislation. And although there are currently no executions, there's actually an active struggle going on to reinstate capital punishment, especially for past and potential acts of terrorism.

So, Russian parliamentarians are indecisive and inconsistent on the death penalty issue. The MPs very often try to

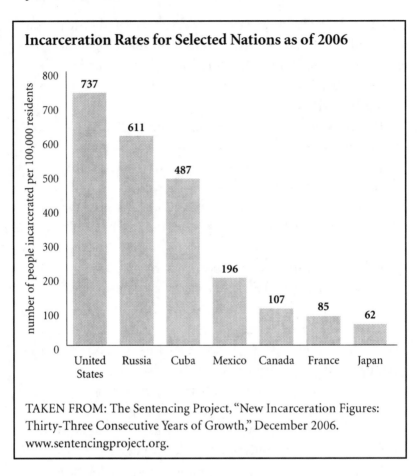

Incarceration Rates for Selected Nations as of 2006

number of people incarcerated per 100,000 residents

United States: 737
Russia: 611
Cuba: 487
Mexico: 196
Canada: 107
France: 85
Japan: 62

TAKEN FROM: The Sentencing Project, "New Incarceration Figures: Thirty-Three Consecutive Years of Growth," December 2006. www.sentencingproject.org.

mask this by saying that it's the Russian people who are not yet ready to accept death penalty abolition.

IPS: Have you carried out any surveys of public opinion on the death penalty?

VS: Last year, Penal Reform International initiated a worldwide project called 'Global Action on the Abolition of the Death Penalty'. This was organised by our four regional offices. Here in Russia, the Yuri Levada Analytical Centre conducted a countrywide poll asking some 1,600 people. We found the majority still supported the death penalty, but not such a high proportion as in previous years.

The results also showed that the majority of the young and educated in the large cities actively supported death penalty abolition. Generally, the number of people supporting the moratorium had increased from 23 percent in 2006 to 31 percent in 2007. Overall, 11 percent of Russian citizens were against the death penalty and we hope this percentage will continue to grow.

IPS: Did you question people on what they thought of life imprisonment?

VS: We did not canvass detailed views on the alternatives to capital punishment. But what we did learn was that the population is evenly split on what punishment is the worst: the death penalty or life imprisonment. This is very important as it seems to suggest that life imprisonment is seen to be as bad as the death penalty.

". . . the majority of the young and educated in the large cities actively supported death penalty abolition."

IPS: Did you find this to be the case in the other countries you surveyed?

VS: I would say this is not just the case in Russia. Most people in the world would have the same opinion. Prisons everywhere are filling up. Over the past three or four years there's been a general increase in prison populations. This is not just the case in poor developing countries, but also in the developed Western countries. And the preference is to isolate offenders.

IPS: You are familiar with the conditions in the Russian prison system. Is life imprisonment a humane alternative to the death penalty?

VS: Life imprisonment has existed as an alternative to the death penalty in Russia since 1992. It should be noted that this punishment is much more cruel here than in other European countries. Russia's 1,600 lifers serve out their sentences in special correctional colonies with a high level of supervision. They are totally isolated from society. One really could describe their living conditions and treatment as torture. When one considers that they can only apply for early release after 25 years of imprisonment, their chances of ever returning to society are really very minimal.

IPS: Are there grounds for optimism that Russia will abolish the death penalty?

VS: Some key politicians, including the president, the chairmen of various committees in the State Duma and Federation Council [the upper legislative house in Russia] including the head of its Committee on Internal Affairs, have expressed their support for death penalty abolition. As I mentioned, the State Duma has postponed jury trials in . . . Chechnya . . . until 2010. This means that Russia's death penalty moratorium is extended for another three years. But I think it is going to be very difficult to extend the moratorium further.

"Russia's 1,600 lifers. . . . are totally isolated from society. One really could describe their living conditions and treatment as torture."

IPS: Does this mean that you think abolition of the death penalty in Russia will be announced before 2010?

VS: Yes, it's possible that within the next two to three years, Russia will ratify Protocol No. 6 and strike out the death penalty from its national legislation. I know that in March this year [2008], the State Duma's Committee on Legislation introduced a draft law on the abolition of the death penalty and this is now being discussed in the Russian parliament.

Periodical Bibliography

Amnesty International "Saudi Arabia Executions Disproportionately Target Foreign Nationals," October 14, 2008. www.amnesty.org.

BBC News Online "Singapore 'Tops Execution League,'" January 15, 2004. http://news.bbc.co.uk.

Economist "The Death Penalty in Japan," March 13, 2008.

Epoch Times Online "Organ Harvesting Still Happening in China Today, Says Report Author," July 8, 2008. www.theepochtimes.com.

Peter Ford "Tibetan Death Sentences Get Little Attention in China," *Christian Science Monitor Online*, April 9, 2009. www.csmonitor.com.

Peter Gelling "Indonesia Upholds Death in Drug Cases," *New York Times*, October 31, 2007.

Suzanne Goldenberg "Texas Execution Plan Defies Hague Order," *Guardian Online*, August 5, 2008. www.guardian.co.uk.

Human Rights Watch "Iraq: Stop Executing Prisoners," May 6, 2009. www.hrw.org.

Human Rights Watch "The Last Holdouts: Ending the Juvenile Death Penalty in Iran, Saudi Arabia, Sudan, Pakistan, and Yemen," September 10, 2008. www.hrw.org.

Dominic Kennedy "Gays Should Be Hanged, Says Iranian Minister," *The Times*, November 13, 2007.

Noel E. King "Death Penalty: Does Sudan Execute Minors?" *IPS Online*, May 29, 2006. http://ipsnews.net.

Robert Tait "Outcry as Iran Executes Artist over Juvenile Conviction," *Guardian Online*, May 2, 2009. www.guardian.co.uk.

CHAPTER 4

Capital Punishment and International Relations

Extradition Treaties Have Restricted the Use of the Death Penalty

William A. Schabas

William A. Schabas is director of the Irish Centre for Human Rights at the National University of Ireland, Galway. In the following viewpoint, Schabas says that many nations refuse to transfer suspects to other nations if those suspects will face the death penalty. Thus, the United States often agrees to waive the death penalty to facilitate extradition. The United States has also had to waive the death penalty to get European nations to share intelligence about suspects. Schabas concludes that to make international legal cooperation easier, the United States should abandon the death penalty.

As you read, consider the following questions:

1. According to the International Covenant on Civil and Political Rights, in countries that have not abolished the death penalty, what conditions must be met for an execution?

2. For what crime did the United States want to try Jens Soering?

3. Of what nationality was Zacarias Moussaoui?

William A. Schabas, "Indirect Abolition: Capital Punishment's Role in Extradition Law and Practice," *Loyola of Los Angeles International & Comparative Law Review*, vol. 25, 2003, pp. 581–604. Copyright © 2008 *Loyola of Los Angeles International and Comparative Law Review*. All rights reserved . Reproduced by permission.

During the negotiations for adoption of the Rome Statute of the International Criminal Court, a small but determined group of States, mainly from Arab and Islamic countries and from the Commonwealth Caribbean, argued that the new institution should be in a position to impose capital punishment. To the surprise of many observers, the United States of America, many of whose national jurisdictions are keen supporters of capital punishment, was opposed. In a defining moment of the debates, United States Ambassador David Scheffer took the floor at the formal, public session of the Working Group on Penalties during the evening of 3 July 1998 to argue that an international Court empowered to impose the death penalty would be doomed to failure because a large number of States would simply refuse to transfer suspects to it.

In a general sense, the ultimate decision to reject the death penalty in the Rome Statute may be said to reflect a growing consensus among States that the ultimate penalty is a form of cruel, inhuman and degrading punishment that is incompatible with contemporary values and international human rights norms. But it can also be explained somewhat more narrowly, and precisely within the optic proposed by the United States. Because it is certainly obvious that developments in international extradition [transferring a prisoner to another nation] practice, as well as other forms of mutual legal assistance, in recent years show the incompatibility of capital punishment with any workable scheme for international cooperation in criminal law matters. Indeed, this helps to explain the exclusion of the death penalty from the statutes of the two *ad hoc* tribunals, for the former Yugoslavia and Rwanda, established by the Security Council in 1993 and 1994 respectively. At the time, three of the five permanent members—the United States, the Russian Federation and China—were enthusiastic practitioners of capital punishment. Furthermore, the territories on whose behalf the tribunals were being established—the former

Yugoslavia and Rwanda—could by no stretch be considered abolitionists. And yet capital punishment was quite simply out of the question.

Extradition Norms Put Limits on the Death Penalty

It is often said that 'international law does not prohibit capital punishment'. It would probably be more accurate to affirm that there is no universally-applicable norm of customary international law forbidding the practice of the death penalty. There are, in fact, many international legal standards that apply to the death penalty, the principal codification being Article 6 of the International Covenant on Civil and Political Rights. Article 6 declares that in countries that have not yet abolished the death penalty, it may only be imposed for the most serious crimes, following a rigorously fair trial, and that it cannot be inflicted for juvenile offences, or upon pregnant women. But there are also four international treaties that prohibit the use of the death penalty. To this must be added the American Convention on Human Rights, which prohibits the use of capital punishment in states where it has already been abolished. Taken together, these treaties apply to approximately seventy States. Moreover, the fourth Geneva Convention, which outlaws the use of capital punishment with respect to the citizens of occupied territories, to the extent that their government had abolished the death penalty prior to the occupation, must also be taken into account.

But international law also promotes abolition somewhat more indirectly. Many States that have abolished the death penalty refuse to extradite or to participate in other forms of legal assistance where this may facilitate the imposition of capital punishment in a retentionist State. This phenomenon contributes to the pressure upon those states that retain the death penalty to reduce and even eliminate it. This is not only a question of state practice; it has also, in recent years, entered into the realm of international human rights law. Important judgments of international human rights tribunals have ruled that extradition in capital cases violates treaty norms, essentially the prohibition upon cruel, inhuman and degrading treatment or punishment. One of the most recent statements on the question appears in Article 19 of the Charter of Fundamental Rights of the European Union, adopted at Nice in December 2000: 'No one may be removed, expelled or extradited to a State where there is a serious risk that he or she would be subjected to the death penalty, torture or other inhuman or degrading treatment or punishment.'. . .

"International human rights tribunals have ruled that extradition in capital cases violates treaty norms, essentially the prohibition upon cruel, inhuman and degrading treatment or punishment."

Europe Refuses to Send Prisoners to Death

As early as 1983, the European Commission on Human Rights held that a sending state would violate Article 3 of the European Convention on Human Rights, which prohibits torture or other inhuman or degrading treatment or punishment, were it to extradite a suspect to a country where there was the threat that torture might be inflicted. Only a few years later, in *Kirkwood [v. United Kingdom]*, which involved extradition from the United Kingdom to California, the Commission considered the possibility that the death penalty, although ostensibly permitted by Article 2(1) of the Convention, might raise issues under Article 3. Kirkwood's application was declared inadmissible, because he had not demonstrated that detention on 'death row' was inhuman and degrading treatment, leaving the question for another day.

The issue returned to the Commission a few years later when Jens Soering was arrested in the United Kingdom under an extradition warrant issued at the request of the United States. Soering, a national of the Federal Republic of Germany, had lived in the United States since the age of eleven. In 1985, when he was eighteen years old, Soering and his girlfriend murdered her parents in Bedford, Virginia. After the killing, he fled to the United Kingdom, where he was arrested in 1986. Besides the United States, the German government also requested his rendition, because the laws of Germany permit prosecution of nationals for certain crimes committed outside the territory. Germany had abolished the death penalty in 1949, whereas in Virginia the death penalty was then, as it is now, very much in force.

In a celebrated judgment, the European Court of Human Rights ruled that extradition of Soering to the United States without an assurance that capital punishment would not be imposed constituted a violation of Article 3 of the European Convention on Human Rights. . . . An essentially unanimous Court held that even if the death penalty *per se* could not be deemed contrary to the Convention, extradition would be a violation because Soering was threatened with the 'death row phenomenon'. In the case of Virginia, evidence had been tendered to prove that those sentenced to death typically spent six to eight years awaiting execution, under harsh conditions. 'However well-intentioned and even potentially beneficial is the provision of the complex of post-sentence procedures in Virginia, the consequence is that the condemned prisoner has to endure for many years the conditions on death row and the anguish and mounting tension of living in the ever-present shadow of death', the Court pointed out. The Court concluded:

> [H]aving regard to the very long period of time spent on death row in such extreme conditions, with the ever present and mounting anguish of awaiting execution of the death penalty, and to the personal circumstances of the applicant, especially his age and mental state at the time of the of-

fence, the applicant's extradition to the United States would expose him to a real risk of treatment going beyond the threshold set by Article 3. A further consideration of relevance is that in the particular instance the legitimate purpose of extradition could be achieved by another means which would not involve suffering of such exceptional intensity or duration.

The *Soering* [*v. United Kingdom*] decision was submitted to the Committee of Ministers of the Council of Europe, which oversees implementation of Court rulings, pursuant to the terms of Article 54 of the Convention. The United Kingdom reported to the Committee that on 28 July 1989 it had informed the United States authorities that extradition for an offence that might include imposition of the death penalty was refused. Three days later the United States answered that 'in the light of the applicable provisions of the 1972 extradition treaty, United States law would prohibit the applicant's prosecution in Virginia for the offence of capital murder'. The Committee declared itself satisfied that the United Kingdom had paid Soering the sums provided for in the judgment, and concluded that it had exercised its functions under the Convention. Soering was subsequently extradited to Virginia where he pleaded guilty to two charges of murder, for which he was sentenced to terms of ninety-nine years.

"Not only do [many countries] prohibit capital punishment on their own territories, but they also extend this . . . by refusing to extradite until assurances are given that the death penalty will not be imposed."

Refusal of Extradition Does Not Prevent Justice

The number of countries that have abolished the death penalty has grown more or less constantly since the end of the Second World War. Approximately two-thirds of the world's

The Death Penalty Interferes with Extradition to China

China has called on Western countries to put aside fears about its death penalty and sign extradition treaties. . . .

Some governments have been reluctant to sign extradition treaties with China because of concerns about its widespread use of the death penalty and doubts about the fairness and independence of its courts, according to Chinese officials and foreign diplomats.

In March, France became only the third developed country after Spain and Portugal to sign an extradition treaty with China. In its agreements with these three countries, Beijing has guaranteed that suspects returned to China for trial will not face the death penalty.

David Lague,
"China Seeks Extradition Pacts in Spite of Death Penalty,"
The New York Times Online, *May 28, 2007. www.nytimes.com.*

states no longer impose the death penalty. Not only do they prohibit capital punishment on their own territories, but they also extend this in an indirect way by refusing to extradite until assurances are given that the death penalty will not be imposed. The right of states to deny extradition subject to such assurances is enshrined in many extradition treaties.

It is sometimes argued before international human rights bodies that if such assurances become a *sine qua non* [necessary condition] for extradition, this may create situations of impunity, where an offender cannot be brought to trial. Of course, such an argument can also be raised with respect to other bars to extradition that have been common for many years, such as the 'political offence exception', and the case where an accused would be denied a fair trial or would be subject to torture. . . .

The Death Penalty Is a Bar to Legal Cooperation

The refusal of abolitionist States to cooperate in the imposition of capital punishment is increasingly manifesting itself in another related manner, namely the denial of other forms of mutual legal assistance. For example, on 27 November 2002, French and German authorities agreed to provide evidence requested by the United States in the prosecution of French national Zacarias Moussaoui for his involvement in the 11 September [2001 terrorist] attacks, after receiving an assurance that the information would not be used to seek or impose the death penalty. German documents apparently provide information about transfer of money from a man alleged to have belonged to al Qaeda in Germany, Ramzi bin al-Shibh, to Moussaoui. French documents depict the childhood and early adulthood of Moussaoui in France, and apparently assist in establishing his connections with Muslim radicals. The Germany Embassy in Washington issued a statement on its Web site:

> The German government will meet the request for legal assistance by the United States government in the case of French citizen Zacarias Moussaoui. The United States of America has assured, that the evidence and the information submitted by Germany will not directly or indirectly be used against the defendant nor against a third party towards the imposition of the death penalty. . . The German constitution . . . prohibits the imposition of the death penalty or any submittance of material that might lead to the capital punishment. The United States government has acknowledged this legal position with the aforementioned assurance.

In December 2002, the European Union reached a deal allowing the United States to get personal data from Europol law enforcement agency on suspects. It was described by journalists as a 'breakthrough' that resulted when the United States accepted that European Union members would not be expected to surrender suspects if they could face the death penalty.

"Those who are genuinely concerned about effective law enforcement, even if they may favour capital punishment ... must understand that the death penalty is an unnecessary—and costly—complication."

The Death Penalty Complicates International Cooperation

The United States finds itself increasingly cornered by its stubborn insistence upon retaining the death penalty. The country stands virtually alone among developed nations, and is ranked with Iraq, Iran and China in what might be called the international axis of state-sanctioned killing. Inevitably, most extradition practice involves those States with which there is a land border. As a general rule, neither Mexico nor Canada will extradite to the United States in capital cases. In the case of Mexico, extradition is now even refused in cases of life sentences where there is no possibility of parole. It seems fair to state that the vast majority of United States extradition practice must now involve assurances that capital punishment will not be imposed.

Those who are genuinely concerned about effective law enforcement, even if they may favour capital punishment for serious crimes, must understand that the death penalty is an unnecessary—and costly—complication. This is true internally, because it burdens the justice system with onerous appeals and post-conviction review. But it is also increasingly the case in the realm of extradition and other forms of mutual legal assistance, as this brief survey demonstrates. The frank recognition by United States Ambassador David Scheffer at the Rome Conference that an international criminal jurisdiction is unworkable if it imposes capital punishment seems also to be particularly valid for national justice systems in an era of globalisation. Abolition by jurisdictions within the United States would certainly simplify prosecutions that involve international cooperation, and make justice in the country fairer, more equitable and above all more efficient.

Ukraine Abolished the Death Penalty Because of Pressure from Europe

Sangmin Bae

Sangmin Bae is assistant professor of political science at Northeastern Illinois University. In the following viewpoint, Bae says that after it gained independence from the Soviet Union in 1991, Ukraine was eager to form closer ties with Europe. High crime rates and instability, however, made it reluctant to abandon the death penalty, which had popular support. By threatening sanctions on the one hand and offering support and encouragement on the other, Bae argues that European bodies were able to convince Ukraine's government to abandon the death penalty.

As you read, consider the following questions:

1. Did unemployment in Ukraine increase or decrease between 1996 and 1998?

2. According to Sangmin Bae, how was the approach of the Committee of Ministers different from that of PACE [Council of Europe Parliamentary Assembly] in advocating for death penalty reform?

3. When did the Ukrainian Constitutional Court rule the death penalty unconstitutional?

Sangmin Bae, *When the State No Longer Kills: International Human Rights Norms and Abolition of Capital Punishment*, Albany, NY: State University of New York Press, 2007, pp. 29–36. Copyright © 2007 State University of New York. Reproduced by permission of the State University of New York Press.

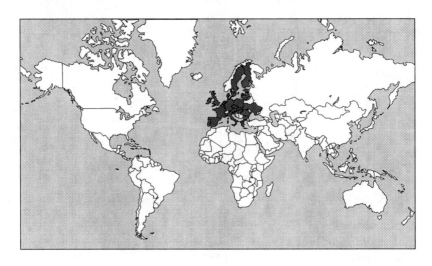

Ukraine has been a member of the Council of Europe since November 1995. Post-Soviet Ukraine's first president, Leonid Kravchuk, and his successor Leonid Kuchma often proclaimed their desire to integrate Ukraine politically into Europe. Like most candidate countries for membership, Ukraine hoped to use the Council of Europe as a bridge to greater integration with Western countries, and eventually to join the European Union (EU). In his 1997 address in the session of the PACE [Council of Europe Parliamentary Assembly] President Kuchma described Ukraine's foreign policy objectives, and reaffirmed that full membership in the EU was of vital importance to the national interest. In the same period, Kuchma repeatedly told the Assembly of the Western European Union (WEU) that Ukraine's strategic objective was integration into European and Euro-Atlantic structures:

> I would . . . like to note that our foreign policy terminology should reflect the principled political line of the state. Along with the strategic choice of adhering to the processes of European integration, Ukraine's firm and consistent line is the line of maximum broadening and deepening of bilateral and multilateral forms of cooperation both within and outside the framework of the Commonwealth of Independent States

(CIS) while safeguarding the principles of mutual benefit and respect for each other's interests and abiding by the generally recognized norms of international law.

High Crime Rate Made Death Penalty Popular in Ukraine

Despite the obvious value of gaining membership of the Council of Europe, it was not easy for Ukraine to fulfill all obligations required by the council. This newly founded nation [which gained independence after the collapse of the Soviet Union in 1991] was understandably hesitant when contemplating an early loss of sovereignty, which they believed would accompany a close association with the Council of Europe. The Ukrainian government was especially unsympathetic to death penalty reform. The classical logic of economic costs, that life imprisonment is more expensive than the death penalty, was one reason. Another important reason for Ukraine's desire to keep the death penalty was that the country had gone through a drastic transition.

After several years of independence, the political condition of Ukraine is described as follows: "You have a government that is weak . . . a parliament which thinks it is an executive and parliamentary committees which think they should be doing the work of cabinet ministers." It was true that Ukraine continued to provide a hospitable environment for organized violent crime. The lid that the government had kept on society, repressing all societal grievances in Soviet times, was blown off, and all social problems spilled over. The rapid political and social transition allowed criminals to exploit a general weakening in the state structure. The growth of crime in Ukraine was a response to social disorganization, increased social differentiation, and social strain. According to the *Den* newspaper in 1998, "Every three years, starting from 1992, the death rate of people murdered at the hands of killers in Ukraine is as high as Soviet army casualties during the war in

Afghanistan. Every day—twelve killings."... Crime rates drastically increased during the period of political transition.

"The fear of an unprotected society in an uncertain political and economic environment made being 'tough on crime' the most important principle of state policies."

As Elliott Currie describes, high levels of violent crime in Ukraine were perhaps generated in part by the radical change to a Darwinian "market society." The society became enamored of the values of material accumulation, yet very few had access to legal ways of obtaining wealth. Universal benefits of the Soviet planned economy, which included job guarantees, regulated wages, vacations, job training, child care, and often housing, were reduced or eliminated. Hyperinflation accompanied the first three years of independence, and between 1991 and 1998, Ukraine's real gross domestic product (GDP) declined by 63 percent (compared with slightly more than 40 percent in Russia). No sector or industry escaped a deep and broad depression. In terms of overall competitiveness, the World Economic Forum ranked Ukraine as the fifty-second of fifty-three countries in 1997; fifty-third of fifty-three countries in 1998; fifty-eighth of fifty-nine countries in 1999; and fifty-seventh of fifty-nine countries in 2000. Additionally, unemployment has become pervasive in the transition economy. In March 1993, the State Center of Employment revealed that nearly 14.6 percent of the people were on long-term leave. During the period in which the process of abolishing capital punishment was ongoing, registered unemployment, let alone "hidden unemployment," grew quickly from 162,000 in 1996 and 351,000 in 1997 to 1,052,000 in 1998.

The fear of an unprotected society in an uncertain political and economic environment made being "tough on crime" the most important principle of state policies. The Ukrainian government thought that the state's strong legal apparatus was necessary and desirable in order to make the transition successful. Retaining a strong criminal policy seemed especially important until some level of stability could be achieved. In 1996, both President Kuchma and the parliament demonstrated that the country was not ready for immediate abolition of the death penalty: "The country's crime rate does not allow for canceling the death penalty," stated the chairman of the parliament during a meeting with an official delegation from the Council of Europe in November 1996.

Along with rising crime rates, another impediment to death penalty reform was the very nature of Ukraine's political transformation. The death penalty was abolished sooner among the losing powers of the World War II—Italy, Germany, and Austria—than among the major victorious powers, such as England and France, which kept the death penalty for decades after the war's end. Experiencing drastic regime changes as the war ended, the defeated nations were able to precipitate legal reforms that might have taken much longer to accomplish under stable governments. By comparison, Ukraine's transition was incremental. Although 1991 was considered to be the dawn of a new era in Ukrainian history economically and institutionally, the legacy of the Soviet Union was powerful and enduring. The former Soviet administrative and political elites retained great power and influence at the center of government in newly independent Ukraine. Because the regime transition occurred peacefully, the entire governmental system was not destroyed and, more important, Soviet-era social and political attitudes and beliefs persisted. As [scholar Paul] D'Anieri and his colleagues point out, Ukraine's institutional continuity fostered stability in the short term, but in the long term it led to a powerful inertia obstructing reform: "Because the collapse of the Soviet Union was accomplished peacefully, there was no chance to completely erase the past and the ancient regime or to start with a clean slate." Even if chaos and violence were avoided in the peaceful process of the transition, Soviet institutions and values have in many respects continued to govern post-Soviet Ukraine.

Ukraine's Resistance to the Council of Europe

The Council of Europe called for an immediate moratorium on executions from the day of accession. Ukraine was also required to ratify Protocol No. 6 [abolishing the death penalty] by November 1998, that is, within three years of its entry. Ukraine signed the Protocol in May 1997, but did not ratify it until the council's deadline. The number of executions actually increased. According to a report prepared by the assembly's monitoring committee, 212 people were executed between November 9, 1995, the date Ukraine joined the council, and March 11, 1997, the date the state signed the protocol. During 1996 alone, Ukraine conducted 167 executions, which, worldwide, was second only to the number in China. Executions were carried out without informing even the families of the prisoners, and the bodies were buried in unmarked graves. Secret executions also continuously took place at a rate of more than a dozen each year.

Noting Ukraine's failure to fulfill its obligations, the Council of Europe officials remarked: "Asking Russia and Ukraine to abolish the death sentence tomorrow would be like asking them to get rid of their governments tomorrow." "I feel I cannot trust the Ukrainian authorities any more," admonished Renate Wohlwend, who was then the Council's Legal Affairs Committee Rapporteur. Among the member countries of the Council of Europe, Ukraine's persistence in conducting executions continued for more than a year after accession. . . .

Public Opinion on the Death Penalty Controversy

As soon as Ukraine joined the Council of Europe in 1995, the death penalty became the subject of intensive political discussion there. Public opinion steadfastly favored the death penalty. Worn down by the chaos of everyday life, weary of waiting for positive results from reforms, and still a long way from an understanding of democratic values, most of the population believed that any violation of the law should be dealt with harshly. With fear and insecurity strong in a society in transition, a prevalent public view was that capital punishment would restrict crime rates. The political and economic transformation, accompanied by a rise in crime, gave rise to popular demand for a strong deterrent. . . . According to a survey conducted by the Institute of Sociology of the National Academy of Sciences of Ukraine in 1994, 67 percent of the Ukrainian population wanted the death penalty maintained or expanded, while 12 percent wanted to make gradual progress toward abolition. Only 5 percent of the people supported the immediate abolition of the death penalty. This opinion persisted for several years; 69 percent were in favor of the death penalty and 16 percent against in 1995; 63 percent were in favor and 18 percent against in 1996; and 62 percent were in favor and 15 percent against in 1997. In addition, most of those supporting the death penalty believed that it should be retained even if Ukraine lost the support of European countries. Among the general public, Ukraine's obligations and commitments to the Council of Europe were not persuasive reasons for abolishing the death penalty. Pro-death penalty opinion is not unique among the Ukrainian public, however; public sentiment on criminal policy has been conservative everywhere, and a majority of the public, regardless of political and social backgrounds, always favors the death penalty.

Ukrainian civil society as a whole is weak and young. The Ukrainian nongovernmental organizations are extraordinarily inactive compared to their Western, Asian, or even Russian counterparts. . . . When Ukraine emerged from the Soviet Union in 1991, civil society was too weak to play any significant role in a democratic political system. Furthermore, ongoing deadlock between the legislative and the executive branches, which seriously hampered reform in Ukraine, made it more difficult for civil society to develop, because a robust civil society at a time of socio-economic crisis was not welcome to the Ukrainian authorities. As [scholars] D'Anieri, Kravchuk, and [Taras] Kuzio note, "Dmytro Vydryn, a former presidential adviser to Kuchma, believes that a fully developed civil society is very inconvenient for the authorities, as it would prevent abuse of powers, authoritarianism, and large-scale corruption." Ironically, two contradictory logics coexisted: Ukraine was initiating a transformation from totalitarian communism and external dominance to an independent democratic system; at the same time, however, it circumscribed the development of civil society to facilitate the efficient and "convenient" transition to democracy. Civil society therefore remained weak in Ukraine. Few Ukrainian citizens belonged to civic organizations of any type, and the major Western nongovernmental organizations operating in the country focused only on fair elections and free media. The question of the death penalty was not part of a public debate. Civil organizations were nowhere close to including the subject of capital punishment in their agendas for action. Domestic pressure for death penalty reform simply did not exist.

". . . in 1994, 67 percent of the Ukrainian population wanted the death penalty maintained or expanded, while 12 percent wanted to make gradual progress towards abolition."

Europe Pushed for Death Penalty Reform

The Parliamentary Assembly of the Council of Europe [PACE] issued a series of warnings, resolutions, and threats against Ukraine for disregarding its obligation. In 1997 the PACE issued Resolution 1112, which demanded Ukrainian compliance, warning that it would "take all necessary steps to ensure compliance" and even "consider the non-ratification of the

Number of Crimes During Ukraine's Years of Transition (1988–1997)

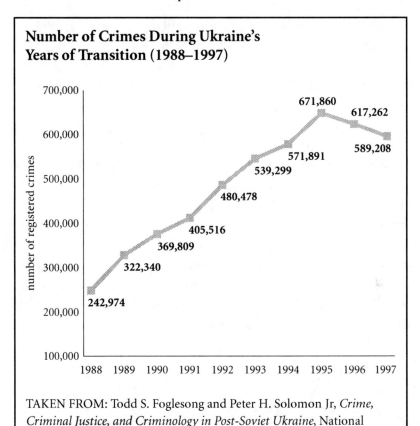

TAKEN FROM: Todd S. Foglesong and Peter H. Solomon Jr, *Crime, Criminal Justice, and Criminology in Post-Soviet Ukraine*, National Criminal Justice Reference Service, July 2001, p.21. www.ncjrs.gov.

credentials of the Ukrainian parliamentary delegation." In December 1998, the council again warned the Ukrainian delegation that the country might not be represented in the PACE in January 1999 because of its failure to comply with the moratorium. The Council of Europe maintained that the Ukrainian authorities, including the parliament, were responsible to a great extent for the country's failure to respect and fulfill its obligations and commitments, in particular those that were to be met within a year of accession, such as establishing legal policies for the protection of human rights, a new criminal code and code of criminal procedure, and a new civil code and code of civil procedure.

Strong warnings were made repeatedly in January 1999. In accordance with Rule 6 of its Rules of Procedure, the PACE decided that the credentials of the Ukrainian parliamentary delegation would be annulled unless Ukraine made significant changes. It also called for the suspension of Ukrainian representation in the Committee of Ministers. Furthermore, the Council of Europe reported Ukraine's "misbehavior" to the major international and regional economic organizations in an initiative akin to an economic sanction against this country: "The Assembly decides to transmit this resolution [Resolution 1179 on the honoring of obligations and commitments by Ukraine] to the European Parliament, the European Commission, the OSCE, the European Bank for Reconstruction and Development, the World Bank, the International Monetary Fund, the Congress of Local and Regional Authorities of Europe and the Social Development Fund."

"All participants in these monitoring sessions might have shared Ukraine's dilemma, since most of them had had to abolish the death penalty some years earlier, also against the will of the public."

In light of Ukraine's ongoing failure to meet its obligations, the Committee of Ministers of the Council of Europe took a different approach from the PACE. Whereas the PACE did not hesitate to issue public warnings and criticisms, the Committee of Ministers took a less aggressive approach, maintaining a continuous dialogue at all levels and collecting information on Ukraine from government bodies, nongovernmental organizations, academics, the parliament, the judiciary, the presidential administration, and the Constitutional Court. The Committee of Ministers held regular, confidential monitoring sessions in Strasbourg, in which delegations from all member states participated. "It was certainly not an easy task to have a discussion on this subject because the majority population in many countries concerned, including Ukraine, was against the abolition of the death penalty. In fact, it was very difficult for our organization as a whole to persuade the government to go against public opinion," stated Johan Friestedt of the Monitoring Department of the Council of Europe.

All participants in these monitoring sessions might have shared Ukraine's dilemma, since most of them had had to abolish the death penalty some years earlier, also against the will of the public. By sharing their experiences in dealing with this subject and emphasizing the fact that abolition would not increase crime rates, the Council of Europe and representatives of member countries had an opportunity to persuade Ukrainian elites to reform their death penalty policy. The Committee of Ministers repeated: "[W]e are here not to criticize you, but to identify with you where the problems come from and how we can help you overcome your difficulties."

Ukraine Abolishes the Death Penalty

Late in 1998 Ukrainian president Kuchma called on the Ukrainian parliament to pass a law removing the death penalty. In September the parliament passed the first reading of the new criminal code abolishing capital punishment. Immediately following the council's fact-finding visit to Kiev in early 1999, when the PACE claimed that no substantial progress had yet been achieved, the president of the parliament issued instructions to the relevant parliamentary committees regarding steps to be taken to honor certain obligations and commitments by Ukraine, including banning the death penalty.

On December 29, 1999, the Ukrainian Constitutional Court ruled that the death penalty was unconstitutional. Based on the constitutional appeal of fifty-one People's Deputies of Ukraine, the Ukrainian Constitutional Court proclaimed that Article 24 of the Criminal Code of Ukraine, the death penalty provision, violated the principle of respect for human life, which is envisaged by Article 3 (the right to life) and Article

28 (the right to respect of dignity) of the Ukraine Constitution; its ruling stated that "application of death penalty as an
exceptional kind of punishment should be regarded as lawless
deprivation of a human being of its right to life." It went on
to say that the death penalty violated "the principle of the
right to life, which is enshrined in the country's constitution,
and contravene[s] the constitutional provision that no one
should be subjected to torture or to cruel or inhuman treatment or punishment." The Constitutional Court added that
"[t]he right to life belongs to a person from birth and is protected by the state."

After the Constitutional Court's decision, complete abolition proceeded quickly. On February 22, 2000, an overwhelming majority of members of the Ukrainian parliament decided
to eliminate the death penalty from the criminal code, the
Criminal Procedure Code and the Corrections Code, and to
replace it with other mechanisms—everything from life imprisonment and hard labor to experimental, New Age psychiatric treatments. Two months later, the parliament ratified
Protocol No. 6 to the ECHR [European Court of Human
Rights]. At the same time it formulated a new criminal code
abolishing the death penalty in both peacetime and wartime,
setting life imprisonment as the nation's maximum punishment. The new criminal code also specified that people under
eighteen and over sixty-five and women pregnant when they
committed a crime or during sentencing would not be subject
to life terms. The new code also introduced more "civilized"
penalties including "public work" as a new form of punishment for less serious crimes: up to 240 hours of public work
for adults and up to 120 hours for minors. President Kuchma
signed the new criminal code in May 2001. The death penalty
was officially abolished, effective immediately, aligning Ukraine
with most European countries.

The European Union Exerts Pressure on the United States to Abolish the Death Penalty

European Union Insight

European Union Insight *is a publication of the Delegation of the European Commission to the United States. In the following viewpoint,* European Union Insight *argues that the death penalty is not a deterrent. It is applied unjustly and is costly. As a result,* European Union Insight *says the punishment is being abandoned worldwide. The European Union, many U.S. states, and the American Bar Association have all argued for a moratorium on the death penalty for moral and procedural reasons.*

As you read, consider the following questions:

1. According to a Columbia University Law School study, what percentage of death penalty sentences are overturned on appeal in the United States?

2. According to *European Union Insight*, in 2006 over 90 percent of capital sentences worldwide were carried out in which six nations?

3. According to *European Union Insight*, have the U.S. states that have abolished capital punishment seen an increase in homicide rates?

European Union Insight, "The European Union: Leading the Fight Against Capital Punishment," September 2007. Reproduced by permission.

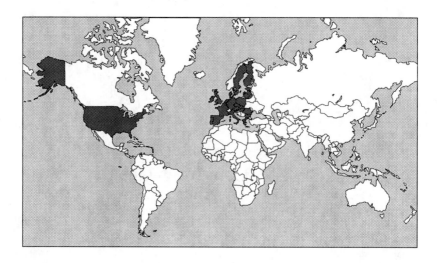

The European Union considers the death penalty to be cruel and inhumane punishment that violates basic human rights. Capital punishment debases the society that imposes it, and history counsels great caution in granting governments power over life and death. The EU opposes the death penalty in all cases, without exception.

Abolition of capital punishment is a requirement for membership in the EU. Under the EU Charter on Fundamental Rights, no individual may be removed, expelled or extradited to a country where there is a serious risk of being subjected to the death penalty.

Capital Punishment Is Unfair, Unjust, and Unnecessary

Extensive research over many years has shown that the death penalty is not a deterrent. It is equally clear that society can be protected from violent criminals by other means. In Europe and a number of American states, a life sentence without parole effectively separates the most serious capital offenders from the general populace.

There are serious practical problems for any country implementing the death penalty. Because no system of justice is immune to error, cases where individuals have been wrongly convicted of serious crimes emerge regularly, even in the most highly-regarded judicial systems. In its finality, however, capital punishment allows no room for error.

It is impossible to administer the ultimate sanction fairly and uniformly. For example, the U.S.-based Death Penalty Information Center points out that in America, the overwhelming majority of reviews conducted in states with capital punishment have found a pattern of discrimination in the application of the death penalty, depending on the race of the victim, the perpetrator, or both factors together.

The high cost of capital punishment is another serious factor. In the U.S., numerous studies have shown that trying a capital case and carrying out a resulting death sentence are much more expensive than a non-death penalty process. Trials are longer, more lawyers are required, and the appeals process is lengthy and likely to result in another trial. A Columbia University Law School study found that 68 percent of death penalty sentences or convictions are overturned on appeal, which often leads to a subsequent life sentence.

Much of the World Rejects the Death Penalty

After considerable progress in recent years, 130 countries are today fully abolitionist either in law or practice. In 2007, Rwanda abolished the death penalty for all crimes, while Kyrgyzstan outlawed executions for "ordinary" crimes (i.e., non-military law and absent exceptional circumstances) and Albania extended its death penalty ban to include all crimes.

Unfortunately, 67 nations around the world still retain the death penalty and, according to Amnesty International, at least 1,591 people were executed in 2006. (Some estimates run much higher, but there is a lack of reliable information, especially from China.) Twenty-five countries put individuals to death last year, but over 90 percent of capital sentences worldwide were carried out in six nations: China, Iran, Pakistan, Iraq, Sudan, and the U.S., where there were 53 executions in 12 states.

The European Union works closely with civil society groups and nongovernmental organizations, and in international fora [forums], supporting the movement to abolish capital punishment.

In 2006, the EU presented a Statement on the Death Penalty at the United Nations, signed by 85 countries, calling on governments to introduce a global moratorium on the death penalty as a first step towards abolition. In 2007, the EU will introduce a moratorium resolution for a full debate and vote in the UN General Assembly.

The European Union also expresses its views bilaterally to countries retaining capital punishment through both general representations, particularly where a country's use of the death penalty is likely to be ended or reintroduced, and individual representations where the EU is made aware of individual death penalty sentences that violate "minimum standards" as set out at the United Nations (*inter alia* [among other things] that capital punishment cannot be imposed on those under 18 at the time of a crime, pregnant women, or the mentally disabled).

The European Union recognizes that the death penalty in the United States has been developed within the democratic process and is reserved for the most violent offenders, and that its application is subject to judicial oversight. Decisions on the death penalty, as on other difficult social issues, are appropriately made by the American people through their representatives in government.

The EU Supports U.S. Abolition Efforts

Consistent with a global stance in seeking a moratorium on the death penalty, the EU supports the many Americans working toward that goal in their own country. A vigorous debate

U.S. Executions in 2008, by State

State	Executions
Texas	18
Virginia	4
Georgia	3
South Carolina	3
Oklahoma	2
Florida	2
Ohio	2
Mississippi	2
Kentucky	1
Total	**37**

TAKEN FROM: Death Penalty Information Center, "Number of Executions By State and Region Since 1976," March 12, 2009. www.deathpenaltyinfo.org.

has been underway for many years regarding capital punishment in the United States, with signs of progress for those opposing the death penalty.

Twelve states have already abolished the death penalty within their borders and none of those 12 have recorded a subsequent increase in the homicide rate. Questioning the deterrent value of capital punishment, Governor Martin O'Malley has called for a moratorium on the death penalty in Maryland. In 2006, New Jersey passed the first legislatively-imposed moratorium, and other states are likely to follow suit.

The American Bar Association (ABA), while neutral on the death penalty, has since 1997 called for a moratorium on capital punishment, declaring (in words that echo the famous dissent of U.S. Supreme Court Justice Harry Blackmun) that "administration of the death penalty, far from being consistent, is instead a haphazard maze of unfair practices with no internal consistency."

Since 2003, the EU has funded ABA efforts to assess the application of the death penalty in individual states. Resulting research has highlighted significant failings, such as: states placing excessive caseloads on defense counsels in death penalty cases; not ensuring adequate access to expert testimony for defendants; lacking proper review of proportionality in death sentences; lack of transparency in the clemency process; and alarming geographical, racial, and socio-economic disparities in the application of capital punishment.

"The EU communicates its views directly to American political leaders at the state and federal level and, when appropriate, petitions the judicial system."

The EU Appeals to American Institutions

The EU communicates its views directly to American political leaders at the state and federal level and, when appropriate, petitions the judicial system.

In recent years, the EU Presidency has made representations to U.S. state governors and agencies when scheduled executions appear to violate certain international norms to be met in cases of capital punishment (e.g., executing a mentally retarded individual) and when states are on the verge of ending a moratorium on capital punishment, and certain other instances.

The EU has also appealed directly to the U.S. Supreme Court, filing amicus briefs in cases including *Atkins v. Virginia* (banning the execution of the mentally disabled) and *Roper v. Simmons* (holding that the execution of juvenile offenders is "cruel and unusual punishment"), and was pleased that EU arguments were taken into account in each decision.

The United States Violated International Law in Executing Mexican Nationals

Kate Randall

Kate Randall is a writer for the World Socialist Web Site. In the following viewpoint, she notes that the International Court of Justice ruled that the United States violated international treaties in failing to inform Mexican nationals of their right to contact their consulate. Randall argues that the United States holds international law in contempt and that the George W. Bush administration worked to push the execution of a Mexican national forward rather than making a good faith effort to respect the World Court's ruling.

As you read, consider the following questions:

1. For what crime was José Ernesto Medellín convicted?
2. Does Mexico inflict the death penalty?
3. How many executions did George W. Bush oversee as governor of Texas?

The International Court of Justice [ICJ] in The Hague has ruled that the United States breached the court's order and violated an international treaty when a Mexican national was executed last year in Texas.

Kate Randall, "World Court Rules U.S. Execution of Mexican National Defied International Law," World Socialist Web Site, January 23, 2009. Copyright © 1998–2009 World Socialist Web Site. All rights reserved. Reproduced by permission.

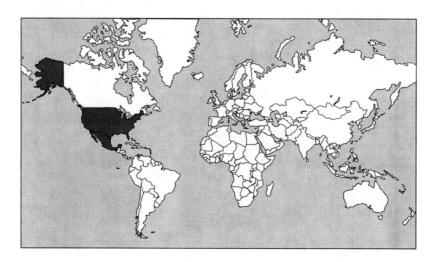

The ICJ ruling confirms the flagrant disregard for international law practiced by both federal and state governments in the US, and by the US Supreme Court. In particular, it demonstrates official American flouting of an international convention governing foreign consular relations and the death penalty.

In its unanimous ruling Monday, the ICJ, also known as the World Court, found "that the United States of America has breached the obligation incumbent upon it under the Order indicating provisional measures of 16 July 2008, in the case of Mr. José Ernesto Medellín Rojas."

"Medellín was executed less than three weeks after the ICJ ordered the US to stay the imminent executions of five Mexicans on death row in Texas."

Execution Proceeds Despite Court Ruling

José Ernesto Medellín, 33, was put to death by lethal injection in Texas on August 5, 2008. He was arrested and convicted in the 1993 gang rape and murder of two Texas teenagers, Elizabeth Pena, 16, and Jennifer Ertman, 14.

Medellín was executed less than three weeks after the ICJ ordered the US to stay the imminent executions of five Mexicans on death row in Texas. In that ruling, the World Court ordered that the US should "take all measures necessary to ensure [they] are not executed pending judgment ... unless and until these five Mexican nationals receive review and reconsideration [of their sentences]."

At issue in these cases was US violation of Article 36 of the 1963 Vienna Convention on Consular Relations (VCCR), which mandates that local authorities inform all detained foreigners "without delay" of their right to have their consulate notified of their detention. Washington ratified the VCCR in 1969, along with an optional protocol giving the ICJ jurisdiction over the convention.

In 2004, in response to a petition filed by the Mexican government, the ICJ—the UN's judicial arm for resolving dispute among nations—ordered new hearings for Mexican death-row inmates who claimed they had been denied the right to contact their consulate in a timely manner.

According to the Death Penalty Information Center, as of October 7, 2008, of the 124 foreign nationals on death rows across the US, 56 were Mexican, including 35 in California and 13 in Texas.

It is estimated that a quarter of the more than 22 million people living in Texas, which borders Mexico, are of Mexican heritage. Mexico formally abolished the death penalty in 2005, and there is widespread hostility among the Mexican population to the execution of Mexican immigrants in the US.

US Authorities Worked to Bring About Execution

José Ernesto Medellín's case was followed closely in Mexico. At every stage, the actions of the [George W.] Bush administration, Texas state authorities and the US Supreme Court served to pave the way for his execution, in defiance of the World

Court's order. With a combination of cynicism and contempt for international law, they worked hand in hand to achieve the ultimate grisly outcome on August 5 [2008].

Following the 2004 order by the World Court that new hearings be held for the 51 Mexicans on death row who claimed their consular rights had been violated, the Bush administration ordered Texas and the other states with such prisoners to comply with the order. While serving the appearance of abiding by the ICJ ruling, the practical effect of Bush's order was to delay any ruling by the US Supreme Court on the issue and stall precedent being set on consular rights.

In March 2005, the Bush administration then withdrew from the optional protocol to the VCCR. This meant that while remaining a signer to the Convention, the US would refuse to submit to international law to enforce it. This signaled the government's intent to flout the 2004 order, which found its ultimate expression in the execution of José Medellín without determining whether the denial of his consular rights had impaired his defense.

Texas Will Not Stop Executions

Texas, which has claimed all along that the state is not bound by international law, challenged the necessity of holding hearings for the condemned prisoners. Following the ICJ's July 16, 2008 ruling, a spokesman for Texas governor Rick Perry commented: "The World Court has no standing in Texas and Texas is not bound by a ruling or edict from a foreign court. It is easy to get caught up in discussions of international law and justice and treaties. It's very important to remember that these individuals are on death row for killing our citizens."

The Supreme Court ruled last March [2008] that only legislative action by Congress could mandate states to hold the hearings ordered by the International Court of Justice. On the

---

Mexico Is Reconsidering the Death Penalty

Calls to reinstate the death penalty are gaining ground in Mexico amid an unprecedented surge in violent crime. Most of the violence is tied to the warring narcotics gangs, who killed a record 5,500 people last year [2008], including a growing number of kidnapping victims.

In December [2008], the governor of northern Coahuila state sponsored a bill in the Mexican Congress that would bring back the death penalty for kidnappers who murder their victims.

Marion Lloyd, "To Live or Die in Mexico,"
Globalpost, January 14, 2009. www.globalpost.com.

---

night of Medellín's scheduled execution, the lethal injection was held up for four hours while the high court considered a last-minute appeal to spare his life.

"[A] spokesman for Texas governor Rick Perry commented: 'The World Court has no standing in Texas. . . . It's very important to remember that these individuals are on death row for killing our citizens.'"

The majority on the court argued that since no serious legislative proceedings were under way either in the US Congress or the Texas legislature that might affect Medellín's case, his execution should proceed.

Two days after Medellín was executed, Heliberto Chi, a Honduran national, was also put to death in Texas. The US high court also rejected his appeal on grounds that his consular rights had been violated.

And the killing machine in Texas continues to grind on. Since Medellín's execution, Texas has sent 15 more prisoners to their deaths, and 12 more are scheduled to die between now and the beginning of April [2009], including four before the end of this month [January 2009].

It is fitting that the ICJ ruling came down on Monday [January 19, 2009], the last full day of the Bush presidency. George W. Bush will be remembered not only for crimes of preemptive war, illegal detention and torture, but for his championing of capital punishment at home in violation of international law and his dismissal of an increasingly revolted world public opinion.

In his five years as Texas governor from 1995 to 2000, Bush oversaw 152 executions, the most of any modern-day governor. In addition to foreign nationals, the condemned individuals included the mentally impaired, those executed for crimes committed when they were juveniles, as well as two women.

Farewell to the "executioner in chief."

Australia Should Work Harder Against the Death Penalty

Michael Fullilove

Michael Fullilove is the director of the Global Issues Program at the Lowy Institute for International Policy in Sydney, Australia. In the following viewpoint, Fullilove notes that Australia, which has abolished the death penalty, attempts to intervene when its nationals are sentenced to death abroad. Fullilove argues that these interventions would be more successful if Australia consistently pressured its neighbors to abolish the death penalty in all circumstances. Fullilove says Australian officials should publicly oppose the death penalty in all cases, and Australia should initiate a regional coalition against the death penalty.

As you read, consider the following questions:

1. When was the last execution carried out in Australia?
2. According to Michael Fullilove, why would it be ineffective to use economic or military sanctions against states that execute Australian nationals?
3. In February 2003, what did Prime Minister John Howard say that Australia's position would be if the Bali bombers were sentenced to death?

Michael Fullilove, "Policy Review: Capital Punishment and Australian Foreign Policy," Lowy Institute for International Policy, August 2006. Copyright © 2006 Lowy Institute for International Policy. Reproduced by permission.

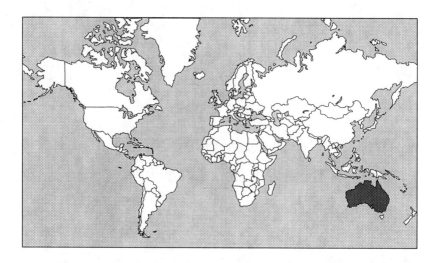

The persistence of capital punishment in our region and around the world is an issue for Australia, and not only when the condemned person is an Australian national. In the case of Australians, of course, the case is black and white. All governments have a consular responsibility to assist their nationals when they are in difficulties abroad, especially when their lives are at risk. Shortly after the execution of Nguyen Tuong Van [also known as Van Tuong Nguyen] last December [2005], Foreign Minister Alexander Downer stated the position plainly: 'We will always make representations on behalf of Australian citizens who are given the death penalty. We will always seek clemency on their behalf.'

Australia's Interests and Values Oppose the Death Penalty

Nguyen was the first Australian to be executed in Singapore since its independence and the first to be executed overseas since 1993. However, he is unlikely to be the last. Currently, at least four Australian nationals are at serious risk of execution. . . .

Furthermore, other Australians are likely to join them on death row. Many of our closest neighbours, including our key source and transit countries, retain the death penalty for drug trafficking and other serious offences. Given the frailties of human nature, Australian nationals are likely to commit these crimes—in particular the carriage of commercial quantities of illegal drugs—and to be called to account for them.

Quite apart from Australia's specific responsibility in the case of Australians facing the death penalty, however, we should also be active on the question of universal abolition, for reasons of both values and interests.

State-sanctioned killing clearly engages Australian values. Opponents of capital punishment make a variety of persuasive arguments: that it offends human dignity; that it brutalises the societies which employ it; that innocent people will be executed because of the inability of legal systems (especially, but certainly not only, in the developing world) to eliminate error and prejudice; that it causes unacceptable suffering to the condemned and their innocent loved ones; that it is does not deter the commission of crime. . . .

"Many of our closest neighbours . . . retain the death penalty for drug trafficking and other serious offenses. Given the frailties of human nature, Australian nationals are likely to commit these crimes."

The Government Opposes Capital Punishment

The Australian Government is opposed to capital punishment. The last Australian executed in this country was Ronald Ryan in 1967. The death penalty has been abolished by the Commonwealth of Australia and all its States and Territories. Canberra [the capital city of Australia] has acceded to the Second Optional Protocol to the International Covenant on Civil and Political Rights (ICCPR), which prohibits the execution of any person within the jurisdictions of the states party to it. Official documents set out Australia's opposition to the death penalty on the universal ground that it is 'an inhumane form of punishment which violates the most fundamental human right—the right to life.' We consistently sign up to UN resolutions calling upon all states to abolish it. Furthermore, at the political level an effective consensus exists that capital punishment is bad and Australia should work against it. Prime Minister John Howard has said 'I don't believe in capital punishment' and Foreign Minister Alexander Downer has confirmed 'the Australian Government has a longstanding policy of opposition to the death penalty.' The alternative Prime Minister and Foreign Minister, Kim Beazley and Kevin Rudd, have stated that Labor is opposed to the death penalty worldwide. The other political parties concur.

"The best position from which to petition foreign governments on behalf of our nationals is that of consistent and strong opposition to the death penalty regardless of the nationality of the condemned."

Unless and until our elected representatives decide otherwise, the settled policy of the Australian Government is to oppose capital punishment. Successive governments have indicated that the death penalty offends Australian values—and as Prime Minister Howard has rightly said (albeit in another context): 'in the end a nation's foreign policy must be values-based.'

Maintaining our opposition to the death penalty in relation to foreigners as well as Australians conforms with our values. It also serves our national interests. Four Australians currently sit on death row and in all likelihood, others will join them there. The best position from which to petition foreign governments on behalf of our nationals is that of consistent and strong opposition to the death penalty regardless of the nationality of the condemned. Such a stance would enable the government to deal with the issue positively and continually, rather than negatively and sporadically. It would increase the momentum toward universal prohibition and bulletproof us against claims of hypocrisy.

Australia Must Be Consistent

If, on the other hand, we create a perception that we are concerned only or principally with capital punishment when it involves Australians, then we open ourselves to accusations of special pleading. Indeed, these accusations are already being made. In the lead-up to Nguyen's execution, for instance, the Singaporean and Malaysian press contained statements to the effect that, as a commentator for *The Straits Times* put it, 'Australians. . . practise double standards.' 'Singaporeans live under the very same laws that convicted Nguyen', stated another columnist. 'Are the Australian government and people suggesting that because he carried an Australian passport, he is therefore above our laws?' Anecdotal evidence confirms that this perception exists in a number of southeast Asian countries. The best way to disarm these kinds of critics is to act consistently.

It is understandable and appropriate that Australia places a particular priority on the welfare of its own citizens. It would be naïve to imagine that any national government would ever be indifferent to the kind of passport held by an individual facing execution—nor should it be. However, vigorous opposition to capital punishment in general is likely to bolster a government's credibility in opposing certain specific executions.

Australia Fights for Its Citizens

If it accords with Australian values and serves Australian interests to lobby for our nationals on death row and pursue universal abolition—and furthermore it is our stated policy to do so—then how well are we performing? The answer is: fairly well on the consular side, and fairly modestly on the universal side.

In relation to Australian nationals, the Department of Foreign Affairs and Trade (DFAT) always seeks clemency for Australians sentenced to death. It takes a pragmatic approach to each case, using the arguments its judges are most likely to find success. In some cases, for example, the emphasis is put on an individual's personal circumstances; in others, on the strength of the bilateral relationship. Generally DFAT prefers high-level political representations to interventions in local judicial processes, unless there is strong evidence that due process has not been followed. Representations are made by senior officials, the Foreign Minister, and on occasion, the highest officeholders in the land. In the case of Nguyen, for example, several dozen written and personal representations were made to the President, Prime Minister and other senior ministers of Singapore by the Australian Governor-General, Prime Minister, Foreign Minister, Trade Minister, Attorney-General, Justice Minister and Parliamentary Secretary for Foreign Affairs, as well as our High Commissioner in Singapore and other officials.

It is not easy to judge the effectiveness of diplomacy that is often quiet. Certainly it is vigorous, as one would expect, and as the political imperative requires. There was criticism of the Government's handling of Nguyen's case, but it is hard to imagine what more Canberra could have done that would have altered Singapore's implacable, clinical determination to put him to death. Furthermore, our consular efforts have their successes as well as failures: Earlier this year, for example, the President of Vietnam commuted the death sentences of Australian citizen Mai Cong Thanh and Australian permanent resident Nguyen Van Chinh after a full-court diplomatic press by Canberra, including personal lobbying by Mr. Howard.

As Nguyen's execution loomed last year, a number of politicians suggested that Canberra should up the ante by interrupting bilateral trade or limiting the Australian activities of Singaporean businesses. . . . These kinds of prescriptions are flawed. They would fail the effectiveness test, as they would be highly unlikely to save any Australian lives. Sovereign governments tend not to take well to bullying, especially by a middle-sized power. They would damage other Australian interests and make us a less effective international player. Finally, their limitation to cases involving Australian citizens would undermine the moral strength of our abolitionist position.

Australia Does Not Push Hard for Universal Abolition

In relation to Australians on death row, then, the Government is reasonably effective. In relation to universal abolition, however, we do less than we should.

Certainly, we oppose the death penalty at the multilateral and bilateral levels. We join other abolitionist states in co-sponsoring an annual UN resolution calling upon all states to abolish or limit the death penalty. At the request of the European Union, which takes the lead on these resolutions, Australia has lobbied Pacific Island countries to join the ranks of the co-sponsors.

From time to time Australia also makes bilateral representations on behalf of non-Australians on death row, usually on the basis of information provided by Amnesty International. Sometimes those representations are made within the context of the ongoing human rights dialogues Australia maintains with China, Vietnam and Iran. Current and former Australian diplomats involved with the making of such representations differ on their value. Speaking off the record, one said that representations are 'very formulaic. . . the point is to make no waves but to be able to tell the nongovernmental organisations (NGOs) we've done it.' Another observed that the making of representations gives the Foreign Minister a story to tell the human rights NGOs at his biannual meeting with them. A third official, by contrast, was more positive, saying the effect of representations is in the nature of 'water dripping on stone.'

Australia Does Not Seek Clemency For Bali Bombers

For Brian Deegan, the impending execution [in Indonesia] of three men convicted of planning the 2002 bombings in Bali is cold solace.

Deegan's 22-year-old son Josh was among 88 Australians killed in the attacks on the Indonesian island. But he is among those Australians who believe their government is undermining its stated opposition to the death penalty by turning a blind eye to the execution of the Bali bombers.

Meraiah Foley,
"Bali Bombers Get No Clemency Plea from Australia,"
International Herald Tribune Online,
October 30, 2008. www.int.com.

He argued that 'a structured diplomatic exchange' can initiate a useful discussion, although it depends on whether the official 'reads it off a sheet or delivers it with conviction'.

In sum, the Australian Government serves in the ranks of the anti-death penalty forces. However the issue is not accorded a high diplomatic priority. Few observers would identify Canberra as a leader in the international abolition movement.

Australia Should Be Consistent

Australia should take universal abolition more seriously and accelerate its efforts on this bipartisan policy issue. There are two steps Australia should take.

1. Be consistent in our public comments

In the advocacy of human rights, consistency is a virtue. The Australian international relations scholar R.J. Vincent observed that 'finding its place in the empire of circumstance is more damaging to human rights policy than it might be to other items of foreign policy, because. . . it is on the substance and appearance of even-handedness that a successful human rights policy depends.' Of course, true consistency is only possible for angels, not governments. No Australian government will ever be as exercised by the execution of someone from Mumbai as it is by the execution of someone from Melbourne. Different circumstances require different approaches. That said, a general consistency of direction is essential.

However, it is difficult to discern such consistency in the recent comments of Australian politicians about the death penalty; instead, we have seen blatant and apparently deliberate departures from Australia's official position. For example, in February 2003 Mr. Howard said that if the perpetrators of the 2002 Bali bombing, which killed 202 people including 88 Australians, were sentenced to death [in Indonesia] there 'won't be any protest from Australia'. The following month the Prime Minister told America's Fox 9 News Channel that he would welcome the execution of Osama bin Laden. In August 2003, the then Labor frontbencher Mark Latham rejoiced in the sentencing of Bali bomber Amrozi to death by firing squad: 'I think it's a day where all political parties should be celebrating, thankful for the fact that one of the bastards has been got and he's going to face the full weight of the law in the jurisdiction where this act of evil was committed.'

"Our political leaders should ensure that Australia's principled opposition to the death penalty is reflected in their public comments."

The capture of Saddam Hussein in December 2003 produced a rare example of unanimity between Mr. Latham, the newly elected Opposition Leader, and his opponent Mr. Howard, who both declared they would not object to his execution.

This kind of inconsistency erodes the abolitionist underpinnings of our stance. It makes us look hypocritical when we ask for our own people to be spared. As a commentator remarked in *The Straits Times* in December 2005: 'Those who are most critical of the Singapore authorities in the Nguyen case are silent when it comes to Amrozi, who is on death row in Indonesia for his role in the Bali bombing which killed many Australians. . . Is this a case of double standards—death for Amrozi because he killed Australians, leniency for Nguyen because he is Australian? Why is the death penalty 'barbaric' in one case, but not the other?'

Opposing capital punishment in all cases, including the hardest cases, buttresses our position in relation to Australians on death row. Our political leaders should ensure that Australia's principled opposition to the death penalty is reflected in their public comments. They should resist the temptation to play to the gallery, even in relation to individuals who have caused great suffering to Australians and in relation to important friends and allies such as Indonesia and the United States.

Australia Should Push for a Regional Coalition

2. Initiate a regional coalition against the death penalty

We need to get our death penalty rhetoric right. We also need to create some diplomatic reality behind it. The Government should signal that universal abolition is an Australian diplomatic priority and devise a strategy to advance the issue.

One approach would be to work more closely with the Europeans, who form the most strictly abolitionist international bloc. Some Australian officials criticise the Europeans' approach as 'press release diplomacy', but it is impossible to deny the impact that their sustained advocacy has had on the issue generally or in particular cases such as the Philippines and Turkey, which limited its application of the death penalty in order to boost its case for entry to the European Union.

However, a better approach would be for Australia to start its work in Asia, the region where we deploy our greatest diplomatic resources and which also happens to be the location of most of the world's executions. Australia has an activist diplomatic tradition within the region and some experience in building constituencies for particular initiatives, as demonstrated by our work on the Cambodian peace process and the establishment of the Asia-Pacific Economic Cooperation forum (APEC). Australia should initiate a regional coalition of Asian states opposed to the death penalty, in order to build on the momentum created by its abolition in five Asian jurisdictions in the past decade. If we make common cause with Cambodians, Nepalese, East Timorese, Bhutanese, Filipinos and others, we will increase our points of influence and decrease the ability of death penalty proponents to accuse us of neocolonialism.

The work of the coalition should be guided by the principles of effectiveness and prudence. The issuing of loud condemnations and the indiscriminate raising of trade and military sanctions would leave Australia poor and friendless, and furthermore would be unlikely to save a single life. Instead we should look for creative approaches to nudge regional countries toward abolition.

There are a number of ways to structure the coalition's work, none of it absolutist in tone. Megaphones need not be employed. We may find it politic to focus our resources on *de facto* abolitionist countries such as Sri Lanka, and seek to move them up the spectrum towards formal abolition. A particular opportunity exists in the case of South Korea, which has not executed anyone since 1998, but maintains a death row of sixty-odd individuals. There is a growing movement in South Korea to abolish capital punishment in favour of life imprisonment without parole, which is supported by former

President Kim Dae-jung and was kicked along this year by the Justice Ministry's announcement that it will study the case for abolition. A similar debate is stirring in Malaysia, led by the Bar Council and a Cabinet Minister. Ultimately this issue will be decided in Seoul and Kuala Lumpur, of course, but a regional grouping may be able to influence the thinking in those and other capitals.

"Australia should initiate a regional coalition of Asian states opposed to the death penalty, in order to build on the momentum created by its abolition in five Asian jurisdictions in the past decade."

Australia Could Use Other Strategies

There are other strategies we could employ, all of them more nuanced than simply demanding universal abolition immediately. For example, the coalition could encourage retentionist countries to:

- Announce a moratorium on executions as part of a move toward complete abolition;

- Restrict the number and type of offences for which capital punishment is imposed;

- Abolish mandatory death penalties (such as the one according to which Nguyen was executed);

- Release comprehensive official statistics about their use of the death penalty;

- Guarantee that death sentences will not be carried out on children, pregnant women, new mothers, or the insane; and that it will only be applied after a fair trial, and when the individual's guilt has been established by clear evidence, leaving no room for alternative explanation;

- Institute safeguards to protect the rights of those on death row, for example the right to appeal to a court of higher jurisdiction, the right to seek a pardon or commutation, and the right not to be executed pending any such appeal.

The regional coalition should be inter-governmental in nature, but the Government could also consider appointing a high-level advisory body composed of eminent people. . . . A high-level advisory group of this kind could generate ideas and provide political cover for the regional coalition.

By being inconsistent and declaratory about capital punishment, we look hypocritical and weak. Stepping up our efforts toward universal abolition, by contrast, would not only be the right thing to do but the smart thing. If we put our shoulder to this wheel, we may even be able to move it a little; certainly, wheels rarely move without pushing.

The Philippines Must Do More to Help Its Nationals Who Face Execution Abroad

Aubrey S. C. Makilan

Aubrey S. C. Makilan writes regularly for the Philippines alternative weekly Bulatlat. *In the following viewpoint, Makilan reports on the case of Reynaldo "Rey" Cortez, who was executed in Saudi Arabia. Makilan suggests that the government gave the family conflicting advice and did not seem engaged in the case. Makilan quotes a representative of a migrants' rights organization who argues that more Filipinos may face death sentences if the government does not work more aggressively to protect them.*

As you read, consider the following questions:

1. According to Aubrey S. C. Makilan, why did Reynaldo "Rey" Cortez convert to Islam?
2. According to the Department of Foreign Affairs (DFA), why were they unable to repatriate Cortez's remains?
3. Who are Marilou Ranario and Rodelio Lanuza?

Reynaldo "Rey" Cortez's life was not saved from Saudi's death row. He was beheaded on June 13. To add to the family's woes, his body could not be repatriated thus, the fam-

Aubrey S. C. Makilan, "Beheaded OFW in Saudi Adds to Long List of Migrants Neglected by RP Gov't," *Bulatlat*, vol. 7, no. 19, June 17–23, 2007. Copyright © 2007 *Bulatlat*, Alipato Media Center Inc. Reproduced by permission. (http://www.bulatlat.com/2007/06/beheaded-ofw-saudi-adds-long-list-migrants-neglected-rp-gov-t)

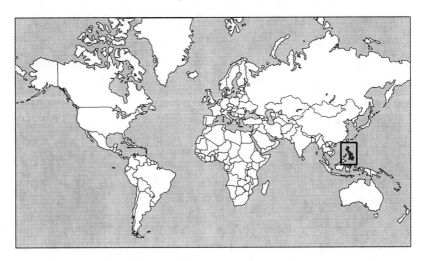

ily could not pay their last respects after missing him for nine years. Even more heartbreaking, the miserable beheaded overseas Filipino worker (OFW) was reportedly buried "unofficial, secret and unmarked," said a migrant leader.

Is Rey another victim of government neglect?

Rey was able to make a phone call to his mother in Sorsogon, clueless that he would be beheaded that June 13.

A few weeks before Rey's sudden beheading, he was texting his family and Migrante International expressing his worries. Rey was sentenced to death after killing a Pakistani driver who allegedly attempted to molest him in 2002.

On May 10 at 6:38 a.m., Connie Bragas-Regalado, Migrante International chairperson, received a text message from Rey which read, "*Kapag di talaga inasikaso ng ating gobyerno ang kaso ko, talagang mapuputulan ako ng ulo. Kasi ayaw talaga ako patawarin ng pamilya.*" (If the government does not follow-up my case, I would really be beheaded. The family of the Pakistani refuses to pardon me.) She texted Rey on June 1 but got no reply.

Although prohibited, the migrant leader said detained OFWs smuggle in their cellular phones while in jail because that is the only way they could communicate with their loved ones in the Philippines.

Just this month, Rey texted his wife Melody relating the same concern.

"*Nagtetext na s'ya sa 'kin na ilang araw o oras na lang baka pugutan na s'ya,*" (He texted me that it may only be a matter of days or hours before he would be beheaded.) recalled Melody. On June 12, she asked the Department of Foreign Affairs (DFA) for any development on her husband's case. "*Sabi nag-aantay din daw sila ng update mula Riyadh,*" (They said they were also waiting for updates from Riyadh.) relayed the dismayed wife.

"*She said that Rey was forced to embrace Islam in the belief he might be spared from the death sentence.*"

Melody told *Bulatlat* that DFA counsel Roel Garcia used to inform them about the results of the hearings on Rey's case. But she lamented, "*Kung 'di mo naman tatawagan 'di mo sila makakausap sa kaso n'ya.*" (But if I don't call them to follow-up, I won't get any information regarding Rey's case.)

When Rey was jailed in 2002, the couple was not able to communicate for a year. She said that Rey was forced to embrace Islam in the belief he might be spared from the death sentence. "*Wala namang nailulong 'yun, napugutan pa rin sya,*" (It didn't help as he was beheaded anyway.) she said, adding that Rey sent them a copy of the Qur'an, holy book or bible in Islam, and other related reading materials in an effort to convince them to convert to Islam from being Jehovah's Witnesses because he believed that it might have a bearing on his case.

In a dialogue with DFA officials twice this month, June 1 and 6, Bragas-Regalado said, the agency's officials seemed to be too careful not to offend the family of the Pakistani driver as they might not pardon Rey. But the DFA officials seemed not to consider how Rey's family was feeling with the slow pace in the developments of the case.

In 2005, Melody said the DFA asked them to stop publicizing Rey's case. "*Sinunod namin tapos ganyan lang pala mangyayari,*" (We followed their advice and still nothing happened.) she said, adding that what she really wanted was to ask media's help to publicize her husband's case and get attention and pressure from anyone and anywhere.

She added that she was given only P10,000 ($215.56 at an exchange rate of $1-P46.39) by the Department of Social Welfare and Development in 2005 and two months supply of rice.

Bragas-Regalado said that even in the reading of Rey's sentence in 2005, there was no representative from the Philippine embassy in Saudi Arabia who attended.

And when Rey was beheaded on June 13, it was Jonathan Panlilio of Migrante International who first informed the family about it. Melody said the DFA confirmed the bad news 30 minutes after.

"*Pa'no na po ngayon? Ano na po bang gagawin natin eh yung hinahabol nating buhay wala na?* (What are we going to do now? Now that the life we are trying to save is gone.) the hysterical Melody asked the DFA personnel who called her. The DFA official, Melody said, hanged up the phone.

Executive Secretary Eduardo Ermita admitted that even the government was "surprised" with the beheading.

"*. . . foreigners who are beheaded in Saudi Arabia are often buried in 'unofficial, secret, and unmarked' graves across the kingdom.*"

Last Request

The Cortez family's concern did not end with Rey's death, however.

Citing a report by United States-based Human Rights Watch, Bragas-Regalado said, foreigners who are beheaded in Saudi Arabia are often buried in "unofficial, secret and unmarked" graves across the kingdom.

Top Ten Destinations For Newly Hired and Rehired Filipino Overseas Foreign Workers (OFWs), 2007

Destination	Number of OFWs Hired	Death Penalty
Saudi Arabia	238,419	Yes
United Arab Emirates	120,657	Yes
Hong Kong	59,169	No
Qatar	56,277	Yes (though no recorded executions)
Singapore	49,431	Yes
Taiwan	37,136	informal moratorium
Kuwait	37,080	Yes
Italy	17,855	No
Brunei	14,667	Yes
South Korea	14,625	unofficial moratorium

TAKEN FROM: Philippine Overseas Employment Administration, "2007 Overseas Employment Statistics," [2008]. www.poea.gov.ph.

She added, "While the Philippine government failed Rey and his family once by not being able to avert his execution, President Macapagal-Arroyo should not fail the family's last request for his body to be repatriated to the Philippines."

"If the Arroyo administration allows this to happen to Rey, they will be complicit in intensifying the grief and heartache already suffered by Rey's family, especially his six children," said the migrant leader, adding that it would be difficult for the family to have a closure and start healing if Rey's body is not repatriated.

In a radio interview, Ermita promised that the DFA would extend assistance to "fast-track" the repatriation of Rey's remains.

However, the DFA admitted that there is no chance to have Rey's remains repatriated citing that under the Shari'a Law of Saudi Arabia, an executed person should be buried immediately before sunset.

More Efforts Needed

Rey is the fifth OFW executed abroad under the Arroyo administration. In March 2005, OFWs Sergio Aldana, Antonio Alvesa, Wilfredo Bautista and Miguel Fernandez were beheaded in Saudi Arabia.

These would just be recurring incidents, however, if the government would not take more aggressive efforts, said Bragas-Regalado.

"Dapat may leverage ang deploying country. Ang problema sa gobyerno after lang sa deployment at remittance," (The deploying country should have some sort of leverage. The problem with our government is that it is only after the deployment and remittances of OFWs.) Bragas-Regalado said. "If they are really sincere in the deployment of OFWs, they will not deploy migrant workers without their protection."

Bragas-Regalado pointed out that there should be higher level of negotiations in these cases and that the Philippine government should exhaust all venues such as diplomatic protests. To protect OFWs, Bragas-Regalado said, the Philippine government should review its foreign policies and that it should enter into bilateral agreements regarding the protection of OFWs with terms beneficial to both countries.

"To protect OFWs [overseas foreign workers] . . . the Philippine government should review its foreign policies and . . . enter into bilateral agreements regarding the protection of OFWs with terms beneficial to both countries."

She also said that the government can even request the United Nations special rapporteur to investigate or even visit migrant workers in jail, especially in urgent cases when OFWs are sentenced to death.

More in Death Row

Foreign Undersecretary for Migrant Workers Esteban Conejos said that there were only 35 potential death penalty cases involving OFWs all over the world when he assumed office in January 2006.

He said that 11 of these cases were commuted from death to life imprisonment through constant monitoring and legal assistance provided by Philippine embassies abroad.

But Bragas-Regalado said that families and OFWs on death row complain that they are not being informed about the developments in their cases. In fact, they said, nobody visits them.

Among the OFWs in death row are Marilou Ranario and Rodelio Lanuza.

A Kuwaiti court sentenced Marilou Ranario, 34, to death by hanging on Sept. 25, 2005 for killing her Kuwaiti female employer in 2004. Her case is now under final appeal with Kuwait's Cessation court.

Lanuza, on the other hand, was detained on Aug. 15, 2000 for killing a Saudi Arabian national. The Dammam Grand Court in Saudi sentenced him to death by beheading on June 10, 2002.

Meanwhile, Migrante International plans to set up a program for counselling families of OFWs in distress. She said they also plan to include assisting children of executed migrant workers to acquire financial support for their schooling in their services and programs.

Periodical Bibliography

BBC News Online   "UK Rules Out Death Penalty Extradition,"
April 5, 2003. http://news.bbc.co.uk.

Dieter Bednarz, Renate   "Bulgarian Nurses Face Death Penalty in
Flottau, Stefan Simons,   Libya," translated by Andreas Tzortzis, *Spiegel*
and Bernard Zand   *Online*, November 9, 2005. www.spiegel.de/
international.

Beijing Review Online   "China Ratified Extradition Treaties with
Australia and France," April 25, 2008.
www.bjreview.com.

Elizabeth Burleson   "Juvenile Execution, Terrorist Extradition, and
Supreme Court Discretion to Consider
International Death Penalty Jurisprudence,"
Albany Law Review, Fall 2005.

Kester Kenn Klomegah   "Death Penalty: Europe Squeezes Russia," *IPS
Online*, July 21, 2006. http://ipsnews.net.

Daoud Kuttab   "The Death Penalty in Israel and Palestine,"
Hankyoreh Online, May 19, 2006.
http://english.hani.co.kr.

Tim Lindsey   "Indonesia's Life or Death Battle Against
and Simon Butt   Drugs," *The Age Online*, May 27, 2005.
www.theage.com.au.

Michelle Roberts   "U.S. Fugitives Caught in Mexico Escape Death
Penalty," *New York Sun*, January 18, 2008.

Spiegel Online   "Italy Calls for Global Moratorium on Death
Penalty," January 3, 2007. www.spiegel.de/
international.

Veronica Uy and Lira   "OFW on Taiwan Death Row Gets Reprieve,"
Dalangin-Fernandez   Inquirer.net, May 4, 2009. www.inquirer.net.

Murray Wardrop   "Mother of British Woman Facing Death
Penalty in Laos Pleads for Her Release,"
Telegraph Online, May 5, 2009.
www.telegraph.co.uk.

For Further Discussion

Chapter 1

1. John Jalsevac argues that Europeans should be more concerned with innocent lives killed by abortion than with the guilty lives taken by the death penalty. Vir Sanghvi suggests that extrajudicial killings in India by police are of greater concern than executions carried out through due process. Do you agree that in general the debate over the death penalty distracts from more important issues of morality and justice? Is it an effective argument in favor of the death penalty to argue that other issues are more important?

Chapter 2

1. Stuart J. McKelvie reports on a study conducted in Canada that suggests that attitudes towards capital punishment affect the severity of punishment in non-capital legal issues. Virgil K. Y. Ho reports that the Chinese have very high levels of support for capital punishment because of traditional cultural beliefs that criminals are wicked and capital punishment is useful as a deterrent. How might you interpret Ho's article on the basis of McKelvie's article?

2. According to Carsten Anckar, what kind of governments are most likely able to abolish the death penalty, and why? Given that Indonesia is a democracy and China is an authoritarian regime, which country do you think has a greater chance of abolishing the death penalty?

Chapter 3

1. In Singapore, a mandatory death penalty law prevents judges from using their discretion in sentencing cases. In Saudi Arabia, judges have vast discretion to interpret the law. Which of these situations do you think results in worse abuses?

2. Human Rights Watch argues that Iran is violating its own legal processes when it sentences juveniles to death in adult courts; the Palestinian Centre for Human Rights similarly argues that the Palestinian Territories violate Palestinian law when they sentence convicts to death. Based on your reading of the respective articles, do you think either of these organizations would approve of the death penalty if it were imposed legally? Are these organizations being disingenuous when they object to the death penalty on legal grounds rather than moral ones? Explain your reasoning.

Chapter 4

1. Aubrey S. C. Makilan argues that the Philippine government (which has abolished the death penalty) has been ineffective in advocating for its citizens that are sentenced to death abroad. Look at Michael Fullilove's article proposing concrete steps to help Australia protect *its* citizens from the death penalty abroad. Which, if any, of Fullilove's suggestions might the Philippines adopt?

2. Based on the viewpoints by William A. Schabas, Sangmin Bae, *European Union Insight*, and Kate Randall, what are some of the ways that Europe or the international community tries to influence nations to abandon the death penalty? Which of these methods seems successful? Which seems less successful?

Organizations to Contact

The editors have compiled the following list of organizations concerned with the issues presented in this book. The descriptions are derived from materials provided by the organizations. All have publications or information available for interested readers. The list was compiled on the date of publication of the present volume; the information provided here may change. Be aware that many organizations take several weeks or longer to respond to inquiries, so allow as much time as possible.

Amnesty International USA
Program to Abolish the Death Penalty, New York, NY   10001
phone: (212) 807-8400 • fax: (212) 627-1451
e-mail: aimember@aiusa.org
Web site: www.amnestyusa.org

Amnesty International USA is a worldwide movement of people who campaign for internationally recognized human rights. Amnesty International USA's Program to Abolish the Death Penalty works to end executions worldwide. It publishes reports including *Nigeria: Waiting for the Hangman, Affront to Justice: Death Penalty in Saudi Arabia*, and numerous fact sheets on capital punishment.

Canadian Coalition Against the Death Penalty (CCADP)
80 Lillington Avenue, Toronto, Ontario   M1N 3K7
   Canada
e-mail: info@ccadp.org
Web site: www.ccadp.org/

The Canadian Coalition Against the Death Penalty (CCADP) is an organization that speaks out against the use of capital punishment worldwide and advocates against the reinstatement of the death penalty in Canada. The organization lobbies the Canadian government to ensure fair trials and to provide adequate legal representation for Canadians convicted of crimes abroad. The CCADP also provides Web pages through their Web site for death row inmates and their supporters to publish their stories online and communicate with the outside world.

Catholics Against Capital Punishment (CACP)

PO Box 5706, Bethesda, MD   20824-5706
Fax: (301) 654-0925
e-mail: ellen.frank@verizon.net
Web site: www.cacp.org

Catholics Against Capital Punishment, founded in 1992, promotes greater awareness of Catholic Church teachings that characterize capital punishment as unnecessary, inappropriate, and unacceptable in today's world. Its newsletter, *CACP News Notes*, disseminates news about Catholic-oriented anti-death penalty efforts. Its Web site includes lists of resources and links.

Criminal Justice Legal Foundation (CJLF)

PO Box 1199, Sacramento, CA   95812
(916) 446-0345
e-mail: ks_temp@cjlf.org
Web site: www.cjlf.org

Established in 1982 as a nonprofit public interest law organization, the Criminal Justice Legal Foundation (CJLF) seeks to restore a balance between the rights of crime victims and the criminally accused. The foundation supports the death penalty and works to reduce the length, complexity, and expense of appeals, and improve law enforcement's ability to identify and prosecute criminals. Its Web site offers reports on pending cases and links to studies and articles about capital punishment.

Death Penalty Information Center (DPIC)

1101 Vermont Avenue NW, Suite 701, Washington, DC   20005
Tel: (202) 289-2275 • Fax: (202) 289-7336

e-mail: cfarrell@deathpenaltyinfo.org
Web site: www.deathpenaltyinfo.org

The Death Penalty Information Center (DPIC) is a nonprofit organization that provides the media and public with analysis and information on issues concerning capital punishment. DPIC was founded in 1990 and prepares in-depth reports, issues press releases, conducts briefings for journalists, and serves as a resource to those working on this issue. The organization publishes *Blind Justice: Juries Deciding Life and Death with Only Half the Truth, A Crisis of Confidence: Americans' Doubts About the Death Penalty*, annual reports about the death penalty in the United States, and information about the death penalty internationally on its Web site.

Derechos Human Rights

46 Estabrook Street, San Leandro, CA   94577
(510) 483-4005
e-mail: hr@derechos.org
Web site: www.derechos.org

Derechos Human Rights is an international, independent, nonprofit organization that promotes human rights and works against violations to humanitarian law all over the world. Derechos Human Rights' Web site includes links to death penalty resources, such as Web sites, blogs, writings from death row prisoners, reports, and articles. It publishes the Human Rights Blog.

European Union: Delegation of the European Commission to the USA

2300 M Street NW, Washington, DC   20037
(202) 862-9500 • Fax: (202) 429-1766
e-mail: Relex-delusw-help@ec.europa.eu
Web site: www.eurunion.org

The Delegation of the European Commission to the USA is the embassy of the European Union (EU) in the United States. It represents the European Union in its dealings with the U.S.

government. The Delegation expresses its opposition to the death penalty to state and local governments. Its Web site includes links to death penalty resources, including EU and United Nation (UN) policy documents.

Human Rights Watch

350 Fifth Avenue, 34th Floor, New York, NY   10118-3299
   USA
+1-2122904700 • Fax: +1-2127361300
e-mail: hrwnyc@hrw.org
Web site: www.hrw.org

Human Rights Watch is one of the world's leading independent organizations dedicated to defending and protecting human rights. It focuses international attention on human rights abuses through objective investigations and targeted advocacy to call for action. Its Web site includes news releases and downloadable reports such as *Iraq: The Death Penalty, Executions, and "Prison Cleansing"*; *Beyond Reason: The Death Penalty and Offenders with Mental Retardation*; and *The Last Holdouts: Ending the Juvenile Death Penalty in Iran, Saudi Arabia, Sudan, Pakistan, and Yemen.*

Justice for All

Houston, TX
(713) 935-9300
e-mail: info@jfa.net
Web site: www.jfa.net

Justice for All is a Texas-based nonprofit organization advocating for criminal justice reform with an emphasis on victims' rights. The organization is a strong advocate of the death penalty, and has established Prodeathpenalty.com, a Web site dedicated to pro-death penalty information and resources. It has also established Murdervictims.com for survivors of victims of homicide.

Lifespark
PO Box 4002, Basel
   Switzerland
e-mail: contactus@lifespark.org
Web site: www.lifespark.org

Lifespark is a Swiss nonprofit, all-volunteer organization dedicated to the abolition of the death penalty. Lifespark's main goal is to arrange penpalships with prisoners condemned to death in the United States. It also informs the public about the death penalty and advocates for abolition. Its Web site includes news about the death penalty, letters, and reports, especially from those who have established penpalships with death row inmates.

Murder Victims' Families for Human Rights (MVFHR)
2161 Massachusetts Avenue, Cambridge, MA   02140
(617) 491-9600
Web site: www.murdervictimsfamilies.org

Murder Victims' Families for Human Rights (MVFHR) is an organization with a worldwide focus on abolishing the death penalty. MVFHR members are murder victims' family members and family members of the executed who are opposed to killing in all cases whether it be homicide, state killing, or extrajudicial killings and "disappearances." It publishes newsletters and annual reports on the death penalty, including *Creating More Victims: How Executions Hurt the Families Left Behind.*

Religious Organizing Against the Death Penalty Project
c/o Criminal Justice Program, Philadelphia, PA   19102
(215) 241-7130 • fax: (215) 241-7119
e-mail: information@deathpenaltyreligious.org
Web site: www.deathpenaltyreligious.org

Religious Organizing Against the Death Penalty Project seeks to build a coalition of faith-based advocates. Nationally, it works with official religious bodies to develop strategies and to promote anti-death penalty activism within each faith tradition. Resources include a compilation of statements of opposition to capital punishment from faith groups, the booklet *Sermons, Homilies, and Reflections on the Death Penalty*, study guides, educational videos, and links to related articles.

Bibliography of Books

Hugo Bedau and Paul Cassell — *Debating the Death Penalty: Should America Have Capital Punishment?* Oxford, UK: Oxford University Press, 2004.

Beth A. Berkowitz — *Execution and Invention: Death Penalty Discourse in Early Rabbinic and Christian Cultures.* Oxford, UK: Oxford University Press, 2006.

Timothy Brook, Jérôme Bourgon, and Gregory Blue — *Death by a Thousand Cuts.* Cambridge, MA: Harvard University Press, 2008.

E. Christian Brugger — *Capital Punishment and Roman Catholic Moral Tradition.* South Bend, IN: Notre Dame University Press, 2003.

Alan W. Clarke and Laurelyn Whitt — *The Bitter Fruit of American Justice: International and Domestic Resistance to the Death Penalty.* Boston, MA: Northeastern University Press, 2007.

Kimberly J. Cook — *Divided Passions: Public Opinion on Abortion and the Death Penalty.* Boston, MA: Northeastern University Press, 1998.

Council of Europe, Tanja Kleinsorge, Roger G. Hood, Sergei Kovalev, and Barbara Zatlokal — *The Death Penalty: Abolition in Europe.* Strasbourg: Council of Europe, 1999.

Barry Dickins — *Guts and Pity: The Hanging That Ended Capital Punishment in Australia.* Strawberry Hills, New South Wales, Australia: Currency Press, 1996.

Hans Göran Franck, Klas Nyman, and William Schabas — *The Barbaric Punishment: Abolishing the Death Penalty.* The Hague, The Netherlands: Martinus Nijhoff Publishers, 2003.

Peter Hodgkinson and William Schabas — *Capital Punishment: Strategies for Abolition.* Cambridge, UK: Cambridge University Press, 2004.

Roger Hood — *The Death Penalty: A Worldwide Perspective.* 3rd ed. Oxford, UK: Oxford University Press, 2002.

Roger Hood, Robert Badinter, and Council of Europe — *The Death Penalty: Beyond Abolition.* Strasbourg: Council of Europe, 2004.

Robert Hoshowsky — *The Last to Die: Ronald Turpin, Arthur Lucas, and the End of Capital Punishment in Canada.* Toronto, Canada: Hounslow Press, 2007.

Dale Jacquette — *Dialogues on the Ethics of Capital Punishment.* Lanham, MD: Rowman & Littlefield, 2009.

David T. Johnson and Franklin E. Zimring — *The Next Frontier: National Development, Political Change, and the Death Penalty in Asia.* Oxford, UK: Oxford University Press, 2009.

James J. Megivern *The Death Penalty: An Historical and Theological Survey.* Mahway, NJ: Paulist Press, 1997.

Terance D. Miethe and Hong Lu *Punishment: A Comparative Historical Perspective.* Cambridge, UK: Cambridge University Press, 2005.

Alexander S. Mikhlin *The Death Penalty in Russia.* London: Simmonds & Hill Publishers, 1999.

Rudolph Peters *Crime and Punishment in Islamic Law: Theory and Practice from the Sixteenth to the Twenty-First Century.* Cambridge, UK: Cambridge University Press, 2005.

Julian V. Roberts and J.M. Hough *Changing Attitudes to Punishment: Public Opinion, Crime, and Justice.* Devon, UK: Willan Publishing, 2002.

Diane Robertson *Tears from Heaven; Voices from Hell: The Pros and Cons of the Death Penalty as Seen Through the Eyes of the Victims of Violent Crime and Death Row Inmates Throughout America.* Lincoln, NE: iUniverse Inc., 2002.

Austin Sarat and Jennifer L. Culbert, eds. *States of Violence: War, Capital Punishment, and Letting Die.* Cambridge, UK: Cambridge University Press, 2009.

Rita J. Simon and Dagny A. Blaskovich *A Comparative Analysis of Capital Punishment: Statutes, Policies, Frequencies, and Public Attitudes the World Over.* Lanham, MD: Lexington Books, 2007.

Robert Turrell   *White Mercy: A Study of the Death
                      Penalty in South Africa.* Westport, CT:
                      Praeger Publishers, 2004.

A. Mark Weisburd *Comparative Human Rights Law: De-
                      tention, Prosecution, Capital Punish-
                      ment.* Durham, NC: Carolina Aca-
                      demic Press, 2008.

Jon Yorke   *Against the Death Penalty: Interna-
                      tional Initiatives and Implications.*
                      Surrey, UK: Ashgate Publishing Lim-
                      ited, 2008.

Index

A

Abolition of death penalty
    attempts, Indonesia, 78, 80
    attempts, Palestinian Territories, 114, 118
    Australia, 191, 193–194, 197–203
    calls for, Saudi Arabia, 109, 110
    calls for, U.S., 166, 179–184
    challenges, China, 141–142
    effects, 46
    France, 20, 24, 25
    global trends, 83, 150, 181
    history, 16–17, 38, 162–163
    Russia, via moratorium, 149–154
    Ukraine, 167–178
Abortion vs. death penalty, 29–35
Afzal, Mohammad, 44–45, 47–51
al-Aqsa Martyrs Brigades, 116
al-Qaeda, 164
al-Shammari, Abdullah, 109–111
Albania, 181
American Bar Association, 179, 183–184
American Convention on Human Rights, 159
Amnesty International, reports, 48, 69, 112, 136, 181
Amrozi, 199, 200
    See also Bali, Indonesia bombing (2002) and terrorist sentencing
Ancient civilizations, and death penalty, 14–15

Anckar, Carsten, 82–87
Appeals
    American judicial system, 57, 165, 181, 189
    British Privy Council, 60–61, 62, 133, 134
    French death penalty cases, 22
    Japanese death penalty cases, 124–125, 127
    rights, 203
    Singaporean death penalty cases, 133–134
    See also Review courts and processes
Approvals. See Review courts and processes
Arbitrary death penalty processes, 109, 110–111, 132–133
Asia, 123, 192–193, 195, 201–202
    See also specific Asian countries
Assisted suicide, 31–32, 33
Atkins v. Virginia (2002), 184
Atonement. See Redemption and atonement
Attractiveness of offenders, 90
Australia, 191–203
    Bali, Indonesia terrorism deaths, 198, 199
    Hussein execution opinions, 199
    Indonesian sentencing of Australians, 78–79
    should work harder against the death penalty, 191–203
    Singaporean execution of Australians, 132–134, 192, 195, 196, 200